Time To Lead

'Succeeding by Helping Others Believe in
Themselves'

Peter Hunter

First published 1993

Updated then republished electronically in 2011, then
re-printed 2012

Copyright © Peter Hunter 1993 – All rights reserved

The names of several of the locations and characters in this
book have been changed as a concession to this litigious
age.

This edition published by Latcham Hunter
Publishing Partnership 2012

CONTENTS

ONE   Leadership

TWO   Do you really want to be the boss?

THREE   Knowing what you are

FOUR   On the way up

FIVE   Self-confidence

SIX   Leader of the team

SEVEN   Face to face

EIGHT   Recruiting

NINE   Tools of the trade

TEN   Changes

ELEVEN   Eureka moments

TWELVE   Conclusions

To Sue - for her many years of loyalty and patience

INTRODUCTION

The key to successful leadership, whether in business, public service, or sporting activities in any area, is an inherently simple almost commonsense task. The myth that it is difficult is perpetrated by those with a vested interest in doing so - those in training, consultancy...

... often those who need to spin an illusion of superiority to justify their own positions.

Having met, worked and dealt with many of those who run our industries and our country - I am not surprised that we have sunk to our current third or fourth rate status in the world and seem destined to fall even further.

Although it is fashionable to blame our commercial and social ills on several decades of decline - attributable often to strong unions and a 'greedy' workforce - in recent years one must count amongst them the outrageous gluttony of those who lead our major enterprises - together with a whole host of 'external' reasons - it is those self-same industrial and commercial management aided by incompetent political leaders that are responsible.

It is arguable that one of the reasons for strong unions is our persistent class system - where shortage of opportunity for youngsters lacking education and openings due to their background - find expression and the chances lacking in a mainstream career through dedication and success in a trade union movement. Do not be deceived by appearances…

… some trade union leaders are very bright and charismatic.

We have somehow allowed an economy to grow that is punctuated by a spectacular unfairness that is based more on background and class than on sheer ability.

The failure or decline of any venture whether it is a business or a nation, must be firstly blamed on the quality of its leadership. To be seen to accept that sort of responsibility is at the very core of leadership. Its lack, especially when coupled with other weaknesses, encourages forces detrimental to the success of a venture.

The management team recruits, formulates policy, supervises its execution, and sets an example to the rest of the team; therefore it cannot evade responsibility for results.

A force such as a union can only become too strong if management is weak. It is an obvious question of balance. A 'greedy' workforce is usually inspired in its demands by the excesses of those it works for, by inadequate justification by the bosses for their own pay and perks. If the workforce is greedy it is invariably following the example of those in charge or exploiting their leadership weaknesses. If those in charge help themselves to a disproportionate slice of the proceeds it has completely negative effect on the motivation of others.

Neither reason inspires any confidence in the people running the organisation.

I have set out to show a practical, simple, no nonsense approach to running a team however large or small. Hopefully you will frequently think that what I write is merely common sense. I hope that is your general reaction, for the truth really is that simple, logic and common sense the responses often solicited from the 'untrained and the uneducated', are the best answers - something all too apparent when suffering the increasing frustration of our rapidly expanding bureaucratic environment.

In today's world, the very word 'management' is as out of date as are many of the policies of those in charge of our society and our commercial life. The impression given of the 'boss class', one of over administration and top-heavy bureaucracy maintaining the status quo, prevail, suggesting a cosy comfortable picture of a lucky few enjoying life at the top.

Occasionally a high profile, charismatic individual emerges, usually an entrepreneur building his or her own business. Such paragons are even more rare in political life. Rapidly attaining celebrity status, they are vital to our lives, providing example, inspiration and, dare I say it, hope.

There are not enough of them to turn around the country towards greater prosperity and influence, and we cannot reproduce such talents at will. The characteristics that make them so successful are generally considered god-given gifts and not widely held dormant embers that can easily be fanned into a roaring fire.

Many acclaimed 'charismatic' leaders eventually turn out to be much lesser mortals than originally portrayed. When their careers ultimately peak, and they struggle to hang on to power, often they become exposed as bullies, intimidators, certainly not the super beings they were originally held out to be.

Frequently their empires crumble, usually on the heads of their 'followers', a result of a failure or reluctance to develop or install lieutenants of adequate calibre, moral fibre, and other qualities necessary for the safe future of the endeavour.

Those rare individuals - the ones with both the talents and the self-confidence to build a team of serious potential challengers for their own leadership position, are what we need, and what we must strive for.

Such a target is only achievable by someone with a sincere belief in the abilities and potential of others, together with dedicated self-belief in how to develop and utilise such talents. This way the very best leaders assemble and stimulate the most loyal and effective of teams.

Having no education beyond the very basic, and no management training of any kind, the early stages of my career were spent in software development in the then emerging world of computing. With software design in its infancy I was able to identify and develop techniques to improve productivity and software quality that are still current more than thirty years on.

I achieved this not through the benefit of education, but more though the lack of it - by not being constrained by preconceived ideas or training. When forced almost inevitably into leading teams and then into running companies, I again approached the problem with a completely untrained and open mind. Prepared to challenge existing, accepted techniques and procedures - I naturally utilised what I considered good practice but sought to challenge and replace all other methods.

This book reflects my views, and passes on to its readers a reassuring formula that should greatly benefit them. It is not a textbook on management techniques.

If leadership could be reduced to a single formula we would all be working for a computer, which in turn would probably fire us and employ other computers in our place - a vision of the future perhaps? This book explores the processes of communication, involvement and the psychology of successfully leading others. It avoids the need to resort to the power of status or the use of intimidation.

By building our own self-confidence and by showing others how to believe in themselves and discover talents they perhaps do not realise they possess, we can improve our abilities as effective leaders and achieve the reputation of the charismatic inspirational leader so much admired.

I repeat, much of what I advocate might appear to you as nothing but common sense. If that is the case then good, you are well on the way to success. However I hope you will merely view such a situation as reassuring...

... a confirmation of your own views and beliefs.

By understanding that, you already know many of the techniques needed to become a successful leader. You are on the way to building your self-confidence and, by establishing a high degree of self-belief, should go on to teaching others how to succeed themselves - thus showing the hallmark of true leadership.

ONE
Leadership

___

The need for leadership is not unique to the human race. It has been fundamental to evolution itself, even widespread and highly visible in many of the animal species we share our planet with. Despite millions of years of such evolution we still retain many of the instincts and motivations of our ancestors, whether on two legs or four, and it is extremely helpful to recognise and understand them.

In the animal world the leader of the pack, herd, or whatever group noun is appropriate normally is resolved on a selection basis involving physical strength.

In essence the ability to fight and win...

Although such an assertive method of leadership selection probably held more relevance in the earliest days of human evolution, it still exists today, from the extremes of a military coup to the more subtle persuasive forces of mental violence found in many social structures, or control through withholding essential information or commodities. As we evolved as a species, leadership selection changed to reflect the emerging needs of the human animal. In early hunter-gatherer systems the man who was the best hunter or who could lead the group to more bountiful territory, would exercise the greatest influence and usually assumed the leadership role. As mankind improved food gathering efficiency through the development of agriculture...

... more time became available for activities not directly linked to survival.

The evolution of superstition into formal religious ritual and practice provided opportunities for those versed in the ceremonial, initiation and healing processes, to gain ascendancy.

The increasing sophistication of tools and weapons provided both political and economic leverage for their makers. Conflict between groups or tribes enabled not just the physically strong and skilled, but also those individuals capable of formulating and communicating military strategy, to influence the course of events and take control.

It is not irrelevant to spend time dwelling on animal and primitive behaviour, psychology and instincts. Anyone who regards him or her as being too intelligent, cultured, sophisticated, or otherwise conditioned not to be affected by atavistic impulses and urges…
… is both arrogant and stupid...

Millions of years of evolution leave instincts far too deeply rooted to be suppressed by education and by social conditioning. Such behaviour is unfortunately, 'in our blood' and by appreciating that fact we are more able to analyse and understand others, something, which is essential if we wish to lead.

EARLY INSTINCTS

Nothing has really changed very much. We retain all the raw instincts but usually choose to disguise them with words presuming higher and finer things.

Who's fooling whom? There is more violence in the boardrooms of London than there is on its streets. It is however a different form of violence - One, which often results in mental breakdowns, broken careers and shattered marriages. It is a violence using fear, stress, intimidation, and humiliation.

Invariably it is carried out by those who would seldom countenance and indeed take steps to avoid violence in the physical sense, yet would unhesitatingly take corporate political steps to oust a boardroom rival irrespective of the cost to the victim's career and mental well-being. That same individual might even take some macho pride in exercising mental violence at this level whilst physically would 'not harm a fly'.

However in the industrial and commercial world of today, many long held attitudes are rapidly changing. The communication explosion means that most of what happens in the world when significant, is highly and almost instantly visible. People are no longer so easily fooled by the trappings of status or the power of a title...
... whether it be duke or company chairman...

More and more we are challenging the right of others to lead us. More and more we see the frailties and inadequacies in our leaders, but do not identify any counterbalancing virtues. We live in a time of great change. Information technology enables the total fund of human knowledge to double every few years...
... that same step used to take several centuries.

In this rapidly changing world the effective leaders are fast becoming those best able to develop the individual talents of those they lead. People who do not run things from behind a big desk and an even bigger job title, but can inspire, motivate, understand and build up the self-confidence of those working for them, and in doing so benefit the corporate or team objective as a whole.

MANAGEMENT STEREOTYPES

Although I am reluctant to label people when we are in reality all completely individual, most company chief executives conform to one of three categories or a variation of one of them.

HEREDITARY BOSS

The first traditional category we should examine is the hereditary boss. Exemplified most typically in royal dynasties the hereditary boss has been a fixture in industrial and commercial life for centuries. Usually descended from someone who long ago started the business, they rule by virtue of ownership and not by ability.

The child or grandchild of the founder or maybe even further descended, this individual is invariably too distant from the original mission or idea on which the company was based. Consequently he or she tends to regard their position as a hereditary right.

The decline of much of industrial Britain from its late Victorian and Edwardian peak can be traced to such dynasties. Fortunately they are now very much on the decline although a similar effect can be found where a strong chief executive attempts to set up a nepotistic succession.

BUREAUCRAT

The most common of the management stereotypes frequently encountered is the bureaucrat. There are so many of them conspiring to obstruct and frustrate almost every aspect of our lives that we tend to accept them as one of life's (necessary?) evils and often do not see their methods as the eroding debilitating tactics...
... that they in reality are...

The person who 'runs' an organisation, using powerful bureaucratic techniques is first and foremost someone who likes every aspect of working life to be subject to rigid rules and regulations. Everything has to be done 'by the book'.

We are talking about a character that always finds it easier to turn down an idea or suggestion rather than accepting it. This can be done either by delaying a decision indefinitely or by proclaiming "it's not company policy".

Having usually risen through the organisation through long devoted service in uninspiring low-risk administration or financial positions, the bureaucrat understands perfectly the network of paperwork, the information flow and structure deemed necessary for the operation of the venture, whether it be company or country.

Change is anathema, to be resisted at all costs, a door through which our bureaucratic hero is reluctant to enter for fear that his established maze of paperwork and enshrined procedures will not cope. Their worst nightmare is indeed one where ideas technology might one-day by-pass the 'system' altogether, leaving him alone a reactionary island that could be eroded into history by the tides of progress and change.

Ideally suited to a world of endless committees and meetings, the bureaucrat affects a profoundly negative influence on surrounding events.

Finding it easier to veto most proposed innovations, when finally faced with overwhelming pressure to agree to change, he or she attempts to buy time with delaying tactics, or by granting qualified acceptance and will call for further research and clarification, again to buy time with which to undermine the proposal or again delay it until the initial surge of enthusiasm dwindles.

Their favourite answer when faced with a problem is; "leave it with me. I'll sort it out"…
… they seldom do…

CREEPING CANCER

It cannot be overstressed how much such behaviour prevails in today's world and how debilitating and frustrating are its results. Not only do we find it in our companies, but in local government, the health service, the police, and of course in central government and our civil service.

It is a worldwide disease. Whole countries, most notable in recent years the one once called the Soviet Union, have been brought to their knees by this creeping cancer of rampant bureaucracy, when it has been allowed to grow to dimensions completely out of keeping with any benefit it might bring. We all experience it in multiple shapes and forms in both our business and our private lives.

The disease is so prevalent that we tend to accept it as inevitable and cease to fight it. We give up. In business, when wielded by a skilled practitioner of the art, it becomes the most powerful inhibitor of change and progress, inevitably leading to the departure of the most progressive and able staff. These, usually leaving out of the sheer frustration of not getting their ideas across and acted on, are inevitably replaced by others more sympathetic to the bureaucratic ideal, and in turn ensure the perpetuation of the system.

I am unable to pronounce too strongly on the iniquities of bureaucratic management. It is the most hideous cancer in the UK and elsewhere, born out of poor communication skills and individual lack of self-confidence.

Assuming a status albeit unheralded, perhaps a science or art form in its own right, it has become a subversive negative qualification enjoyed by far too many.

Endemic for centuries, its exponents operated from the inherited base of a deep-rooted and well-established culture. However we who aspire to be the more successful leaders of the future must understand very well its strength and extent as well as its techniques, as it is likely to be one of the single most powerful external obstructions to our own progress.

PETER PRINCIPLE

Aligned very closely and generally coexisting with ingrained bureaucratic management, is the phenomenon best highlighted by the well-known views and observations of Dr L J Peter, popularly embodied in the 'Peter Principle'.

For the benefit of anyone unlikely enough not to be familiar with it, the principle can be broadly expressed as follows; 'within an organisation people who are good at their job are sooner or later promoted. This process continues until they are promoted into a position in which, for one reason or another they are not effective.

This tends to restrict their further promotion, and they tend to therefore remain in that ineffective position, functioning poorly, and essentially blocking the promotion of others more able to do the job. They have reached their "level of incompetence", and tend to stay there, often until retirement.

By promoting staff until their level of incompetence is reached, most or all of the senior positions in an organisation could become filled with individuals that are out of their depth, with obvious disastrous results.

I suspect we all know of organisations where this has occurred.

Look around and you will see that the 'Peter Principle' remains alive and thriving. Couple it with the bureaucratic style of management, its compatible and very willing bed-fellow, and one wonders if there is any hope for those who set out to become the engineers of change.

CHARISMATIC - INSPIRATIONAL

Finally in our catalogue of the most identifiable management stereotypes, is the leader best described as 'charismatic, leading from the front, entrepreneurial, open, inspirational etc. The rarest of the three stereotypes, such individuals become rapidly disillusioned and frustrated by a traditional career path, leading to an early venture into setting up their own businesses.

Although numerically the rarest of my three categories, such people often achieve spectacular and well publicised success, and are soon elevated to celebrity status by the media.

Unfortunately such media attention tends to then concentrate on their social habits and on their extravagant consumerism, rather than on the commercial virtues and business skills contributing to their success, thus depriving the population in general of a constructive insight into really useful ideas, techniques and policies.

One of the problems facing many businesses and organisations in the public domain is how to attract and hold this category of leader. Those most naturally conforming to this stereotype gain the bulk of their motivation from working for themselves therefore employing them tends to be a futile task. Their restless and impatient natures merely signal the day when they will depart to do their own thing.

Far more can be gained by cultivating some of the techniques of the charismatic leader amongst the workforce in general. Although unlikely to produce a nation of self-employed multimillionaires, such a process will widely upgrade leadership skills and make serious inroads into our existing ranks of management.

IDEAL LEADERS

It is perhaps too easy to criticise those we have worked for and worked with. Everyone falls short of the ideal. It is more difficult to define what is ideal when it comes to the one we would like to see running our companies…
… our economy our affairs…

Obviously we tend to be very subjective in our portrayal of the most desired leadership qualities. However we must have a role model on which to base our target for the purposes of this book. My ideal leader for this purpose is as follows:

Firstly, and of great importance, is the leader's loyalty to the team. From this and from the other attributes which I catalogue below, comes the mutual loyalty so essential to any team venture. The capacity of the one in charge to inspire and maintain such a mutual loyalty coupled with respect for each other, are the fundamentals of corporate and team success.

To foster this primary objective I expect the leader to be highly, and visibly decisive, showing a high degree of personal self-confidence. In the decision-making role much of the decisions are in reality the authorisation, the endorsement of recommendations made by team members. What is vitally necessary is to take immediate responsibility when things go wrong.

The team member should never be blamed even if it is his or her recommendation that has gone wrong, as the responsibility is always that of the leader. However the team should receive the praise when its ideas or recommendations bring success. The ideal leader is the last to claim the credit…
… It should always be attributed to the team…

INSPIRE AND MOTIVATE

The person running things must be able to inspire and motivate the team, particularly in adversity. Receptive to their ideas, listening to their complaints, their problems, hopes and aspirations, the role is often that of a catalyst in helping those ideas to mature, and also in creating synergy between the team members.

He or she is able to maintain the team's objectivity during fulfilment of the mission, relentlessly and with determination. Acting as a buffer between the team and the 'customer base' to smooth out problems and minimise tensions. Communication skills are obviously vital as is an analytical approach to 'insurmountable' problems.

Protect the team from corporate politics, whilst weeding out any politics within the team. Never bowing to crude pressure, whilst retaining a sense of what is practical. Able to modify policy rapidly and decisively in 'real-time', especially when faced with a set of unforeseen circumstances or some random disaster.

Understanding individuality and delegating openly, explaining the reasons for structuring the project in such a way - one of the first to recognise a wrong decision, and the very first to rectify it.

The person in charge should be willing himself or herself to undertake the most unpleasant tasks rather than delegate them, and be willing to delegate the best assignments. Ready to solve any irretrievable personnel problems with a decisive and timely dismissal, whilst being the first to accept responsibility for what was probably a recruiting error that caused it.

RESPECT

The boss should not seek to be liked - respect is enough. He or she must always be fair and honest. Willing to fight like a tiger for the interests of the team, but also respecting and cultivating similar qualities in those reporting to him or her.

He is hopefully charismatic, and quite possibly 'larger than life' in some aspects of personal appearance, outside of work activities, life-style or history.

Preferably he is someone with a 'reputation'. Above all capable of inspiring others, generating tremendous enthusiasm, stimulating mutual loyalty, and showing the team and its members how to believe in themselves, their mission objectives, and the planned way of achieving them. The very best leaders create a feeling of excitement amongst those they lead.

KEY POINTS

*   Understanding others - the key to leadership
*   Negative attitudes kill growth and change
*   Bureaucracy - a creeping cancer
*   Misguided ambitions can create incompetence
*   Self-made millionaires upgrade leadership
*   Mutual loyalty essential to team leadership
*   Face up to unpleasant tasks - delegate the best assignments
*   Do not expect to be liked - respect is what is important
*   Be 'exciting' to others

TWO
Do You Really Want To Be The Boss?

One of the most interesting and enjoyable functions of my business career has been recruiting. Interviewing potential colleagues is a stimulating and fascinating business. It serves not only to build, or to restructure your team, thus presenting opportunities to improve and extend it, but, if you approach the task correctly it provides you with a superb opportunity to reconsider many aspects of what you are intending to achieve. However there will be more lately, in another chapter, about the recruitment process.

A regular item arising during an interview is what are the applicant's career ambitions. Most candidates at the level I interview express considerable ambition, often aspiring to at least a directorship and more usually wanting to run a sizeable division, large department or a small or medium sized company.

Inevitably it has become part of our current commercial culture for a job applicant to express such ambitions. Job-seekers would, at least in the positions for which I had recruitment responsibility, not wish to be seen as aiming lower lest they appear to lack the required ambition, drive and self-confidence for the position which they are applying for.

Because the above response is such a standard one I invariably follow it with a supplementary question. I ask the candidate what he or she thinks being the boss means in the context of why they want to be it, and what does it actually involve? This supplementary question usually exposes the answer to the original question as merely glib and predictable.

Few of these aspiring captains of industry think through the true functions and responsibilities of the job. The obvious attractions of high salary, the perks and apparent power are the overriding concerns and very little thought seems to be expended on the 'down-side' aspects of leadership.

Most employees believe that they can perform better than the people that run the organisation, and tend to romanticise the boss's role into a comfortable lifestyle of long business lunches, expensive cars and other benefits.

Anyone with serious ambitions to lead others should think very carefully about what is involved before expending too much effort in following such a path.

Far too many end up totally out of their depth in middle or even top management jobs, usually to the detriment of their own health and happiness and to the company's efficiency. They could often be more contented, more useful, and may ultimately become more prosperous in a position 'lower' in the organisation...
... one more suited to their abilities and temperament...

EVERYONE IS GOOD AT SOMETHING

Everyone has some form of talent. It is one of the tragedies of modern life that so many of us spend unhappy working lives because we are insufficiently motivated or simply do not enjoy our work. As such a large proportion of our lives is spent in the workplace, it is a great waste of our time on earth if we do not find our employment fulfilling. It goes without saying that if everyone could achieve satisfaction at work then our society would be far more pleasant, in addition to being a much more efficient and prosperous place.

In the early days of the computer software industry it was very common for a programmer who was very good at his or her job, to be rapidly promoted to a supervisory or managerial position. The fact is the skills of designing and coding good software have very little to do with effective project management or the leadership of a team of highly technical people. To promote someone on such an irrelevant basis is a recipe for disaster, which still gets repeated again and again…
… we learn so slowly…

It took many years before it was generally realised that software development could itself be a very satisfying life-time career, and not just a transient phase on the way to systems design or towards 'management'.

Of course the computer industry is not the only sector where people feel the pressure to get themselves promoted out of perfectly well-paid and satisfying roles into years of misery as ineffective managers, or for their bosses to assume that technical skills equate to leadership ability. It is a common phenomenon but none the less a deadly one for an industrialised society.

WHAT IS YOUR PAIN THRESHOLD?

This probably is the first question you should ask yourself when contemplating life as a chief executive. Whatever the quality of the team being led, the role of the real leader is invariably a very lonely one.

If the solitude of decision-making is not keenly felt, I suspect we are referring to an individual who is merely carrying out a policy laid down by some superior body such as the board of a holding company, rather than being truly in charge of the operation.

Although in reality most of us have to report to someone unless of course we hold all the equity in the company, the test of our operational autonomy is reflected by the extent that 'the buck stops here'...
... to quote a famous American president.

Responsibility is tough. I would misrepresent the facts to suggest otherwise. Forget the long hours and the forfeiture of holidays. They are often mythical sacrifices engineered mainly for PR or staff relation reasons.

Where they exist they are a dubious virtue whose value is discussed later in this book. Often they are a cover-up for a lack of flair and ability in the management function, a substitute for true talent. The only things that can be used by an individual to distinguish performance form that of colleagues...
... often a solitary 'claim to fame'...

Workaholics are in my view suspect. Feeling it important to be the first into the office and the last out, might at first seem impressive but it has very little to do with true leadership where the quality of the effort is far more important than the quantity.

Such work habits indicate amongst other things an inability or reluctance to delegate, and leave little spare capacity for emergencies and for troubleshooting...

... at best they show insecurity...

EMERGENCY RESERVE

Everyone needs a reserve of nervous energy and emotional concentration to summon up in times of exceptional need. Attempting to work flat-out all the time soon destroys this emergency reserve and can leave an individual sadly lacking when inspired leadership is most required.

At best the workaholic is attempting to set an example to subordinates and by doing so increase the length of their working hours. The old adage about 'all work and no play make Jack a dull boy' has many a truth. We all need to relax, to play, and enjoy ourselves in pastimes outside our jobs.

Performing well at things other than work helps relieve stress and often restores a sense of balance to our overall outlook. Feeling the need to work all hours indicates either that you employ the wrong team or that you are insecure as their leader.

Being the boss means taking responsibility for the success of others, and by doing so assuming accountability for their general well being. Our careers in most cases, determine our standard of living and certainly affects the quality of our lives.

If taken seriously (and it should never be taken in any other way), being the boss, leading or being 'in charge' of others is an awesome responsibility.

Think about it! Too many bosses view far too lightly the effect they have on their employee's working lives, and consequently their life outside the working environment. I know that in many cases employees 'vote with their feet' leaving to go to a more acceptable job, but that in itself can be traumatic for everyone concerned.

PRESSURE FROM ALL DIRECTIONS

The quality of one's team however high, does not guarantee a stress-free life for the person in charge. Running a commercial operation must be profitable. It will not survive otherwise.

Even if the organisation exists in order to provide a public service or is part of local or central government, then it should still be measured by commercial parameters of efficiency - in effect, a 'profit oriented' approach. In all cases there must be or should be, on-going pressure for the operation to be 'profitable'.

The trading company operating in a competitive market is only viable if profitable. The continued employment of its staff depends on the organisation's efficiency, as does the financing of future development and long-term investment.

Increasingly commercial yardsticks are measuring the size, performance, and direction of tax-funded institutions such as health-care and subsidised public transport. Consequently the leadership of such organisations are coming under similar pressures to those in the commercial sectors, and will increasingly compete for the best leadership skills.

ENDLESS GAME

The pressures to run a profitable venture must therefore be relentless. In addition to its importance in the survival of commercial organisations living in competitive markets, profitability has a more short-term role in the rewarding and motivation of quality personnel.

It is an endless game - one that builds increasing pressure on the person at the helm. However comfortable we are with such pressure in the early days of our leadership, continual repetition year after year after year will inevitably have a cumulative and eroding effect both on personal morale, job satisfaction and self-motivation.

Running a business means taking responsibility for providing the shareholders with a satisfactory return on their investment. This can be income, capital gain, or a mixture of both. Obviously many shareholders need income on a regular basis in order to survive.

Most businesses embody an on-going struggle between the call for current profitability and the need to finance long-term growth. This is often a very real conflict and one, which can be remarkably difficult to reconcile.

In its most pronounced form we often see shareholders enjoying the high profits derived from a 'mature product', one in which the development and initial marketing costs have long been recovered.

Mature products or established services; often enjoy many more years of success. These are then overtaken by new development or by competitors recognising a good thing, replicating the product or service and eroding the market share of the originator.

There is a tendency for many organisations to sit back on their laurels and enjoy the success of such products readily 'milking' the cash generated. Although this is a well-known and often fatal corporate disease…

… it is still far too common...

SHORT TERM PROFIT ADDICTION

Unfortunately shareholders become too easily addicted to high dividends and to the capital appreciation of their holdings. They often resist short-term profit dilution in order to fund the necessary continuous development of new products, services and markets. This apparent conflict of interest puts enormous pressures on a chief executive.

The shareholders want their short-term profits. They also want a high share price. Often assuming that the company must be developing the new products, services, markets etc., necessary for its longer term success, they remain reluctant to forgo current profits to fund the future. They are also sometimes resistant to injecting more capital into the business to fund research and development of products and markets.

Those working in the company require and should get good salaries if it is doing well. They are seldom sympathetic to accepting lower wages to finance development yet they will be among the first, quite rightly, to complain if the growth and development which ensures their future and adds interest to their careers...
… is not taking place...

Add to the above cocktail some important external influences such as economic recession, changing world markets for products and commodities, currency exchange fluctuations, revised legislation affecting employment and products, shortage of skilled staff, industrial relation problems, interest rates etc, and it can quickly be seen that running an organisation is not all wine and roses.

Do you still want to do it? Are you still sure you can do it and do it well?

STRESS - EVEN WHEN THINGS ARE GOING WELL

Even when things appear to be going particularly well pressures and stresses will abound. Success generally brings about even further pressure for growth.

Often the required expansion is achieved by the acquisition of other companies, consequently providing opportunities for consolidation and re-structuring, which in turn leads to both redundancies and migration of key staff who believe their own chances of promotion are being curtailed.

Sometimes the boss will spend many years grooming and developing the careers of particularly able subordinates only to see them enticed away by competitors, or leaving to set up their own businesses. This can be an extremely painful experience for the mentor as inevitably bonds have been formed with colleagues, and their loss to the team can be an emotional one as well as expensive and time consuming to rectify.

Inevitably employment termination, either redundancy or dismissal due to incompetence, can affect all but the most insensitive. It provides a fertile ground for all manner of stress related problems.

Many instances exist where chief executives have been incapable of making mass redundancies when circumstances have dictated them, and have had to move aside whilst others carried out the deed. Invariably and justifiable they themselves then become another of the redundancies. Continual undertaking of tasks which an individual finds personally unpleasant, particularly if they involve having to dismiss a friend or a long-standing colleague, can lead to depression related illnesses and other health hazards such as high blood pressure and cardiac problems.

Do not expect or seek to be liked, but aim to be respected. If you need to be popular you are unsuited for life at the top of industry or commerce.

BOARD-ROOM DISPUTES

The boardroom can be an extremely violent place in the mental rather than the physical sense. Whilst our aspiring leaders will, once having risen to the heights of a chief executive, be able to influence a very high degree of control on the composition of their board, things are unlikely to be so ideal on the way up. We are competitive animals, and by the nature of competition the most successful will be clustered around the top.

I hope no one reading this book will be so naive as to imagine that rising to the top of any sizeable organisation can be achieved without a fight. Vital requirements consist of corporate political skills, assertiveness, animal cunning, and the capability of raw mental aggression.

Being good at one's job is only part of the picture and often not the most important part. The person at the top is usually a tough animal and must not be underestimated by aspiring successors. The ability to survive tactics that exploit personal weaknesses, whether they are financial or aspects of character will only help to achieve reaching the top position.

Past mistakes, career setbacks and misdemeanours, will be trawled up for public consumption, aired by colleagues with no respect for your reputation. Rivals will 'set you up' by seeking to divert you into soul-destroying, difficult, sometimes almost impossible assignments. Intimidation and humiliation will be attempted, and personal abuse and insult occasionally used.

Alliances will be formed, broken and then re-established. Long-serving careers may be casually destroyed. In this corporate battlefield, if necessary a real or imagined competitor can be driven into a nervous breakdown or an even worse health problem, if they are not first forced to leave the organisation.

The boardroom can be a lively and exciting place, making a military firefight seem almost tame by comparison. Learn from it, and resolve to build your own team as free from internal politics as is humanly possible. Channel all the aggressive and competitive elements into fighting the company's external competition...

...There is always more than enough of that to deal with...

I realise maybe I have painted a somewhat pessimistic picture. Unfortunately I have seen too many lives ruined by ability, greed, and ambition leading to an uncomfortable career in a senior position. A misfit of talent resulting in ruined health and shattered marriages

The money, the glamour, and above all, the power, can be alluring and tantalising prizes. However the price is very high and only a few can readily afford it in terms of the wear and tear on their physical and mental well-being. For many it may be better to be satisfied with a rewarding but less demanding job.

Think very carefully before you make too great a commitment. Having considered it all, if you still really want to get to the top then you probably have many of the necessary qualities.

KEY POINTS

*   Being the boss is lonely and can kill
*   Over work is a substitute for flair, ability, and talent
*   Responsibility for the success and well-being of others - the leader's job
*   Profit pressures erode morale and self-motivation
*   Complacency is fatal - a corporate disease
*   Product development for long-term growth
*   Growth through acquisition leads to redundancies
*   The chief executive - tough animal in a violent boardroom

THREE
Knowing What You Are

Although I am not a golfer, I approach most of life applying the practicalities of the game of golf. As I see it the objective of the game is to ideally complete the course of eighteen holes in a total of eighteen strokes.

A round in eighteen! This of course should then be repeated in every game. I am reliably informed that this has never yet been accomplished and probably never will be. An actual hole-in-one is apparently a rarity, unlikely to be achieved by the average golfer, and probably a once in a lifetime high for just a select few...
... a cause for great celebration...

THE GOLF PRINCIPLE

My personal attitude to complex or difficult tasks and projects has always reflected the golfer's practical approach - that it is unrealistic to plan on getting a hole in one every time. However the objective of the exercise involves trying to do precisely that.

What is important is that each stroke increases the chances of the next one succeeding in the objective of putting the ball into the hole. That is how progress is made. That is how one aims to win, not by absolute perfection, but by cultivating a higher ratio of success than one's competitors.

In reality life is a succession of iterations, each progressing in the direction of ultimate success, and each one increasing the 'player's chance of getting there with the next move.

Many projects and ventures in life conform to the golf analogy. Most of us know in what broad area our final objective lies. We would naturally like to get there in one easy move but realise it is not totally practical to expect to do so. Therefore if we are intelligent or if we apply common sense, we accept the necessity for a certain degree of patience. We then again move forward, each action hopefully a meaningful one, in the general direction of our final goal, each successive move increasing our chances of success.

A PRACTICAL APPLICATION

Finding myself suddenly in charge of a troubled software house some twenty plus years ago, I discovered the structured approach provided by the golf principle invaluable in sorting out one of the company's major problem areas. Our product was the development of computer systems to a fixed price - projects contracted to be completed by an agreed deadline.

Drawing from construction industry practice we were agreeing to pay a financial penalty for late delivery. All the systems were original and highly individual (we were not in the business of re-inventing the wheel). Consequently we had no historical database upon which to draw for estimating purposes. However we were regularly committing ourselves to very large projects quoting a fixed-price and guaranteeing the completion date.

In addition was of course the liability of the penalty clause if we fell short of these commitments - plus additional guarantees relating to the quality of the software. Everything was based on estimates that were often little more than inspired guesses usually slimmed down to make the total price 'more competitive'.

No wonder the company was losing money on almost every project. Mainframe computer systems designed specifically for an individual application are today still problematic. They were even more so in the 1960's and 1970's when there were not so many design tools and productivity aids in existence as there are now. Large systems development was a major task despite the availability of staff of a much higher average level of ability than are available today.

We were quite literally 'betting the company' on the successful outcome of the larger projects - slowly bleeding it to death on smaller ones. The ineffective estimating techniques and lack of project management tools wee having a deleterious effect on the systems design and programming teams - the ones who had to do the hard work.

Often it was the team who would be blamed for taking longer to carry out the work than the estimates allowed for. As each weekly project status report showed the project becoming more and more behind schedule and over-budget, the staff would grow more demoralised and productivity would then deteriorate further.

A vicious circle would then emerge, productivity spiralling downwards and the deviation from the budget and schedule becoming even greater. The reason for this decline in output was of course obvious. The project team did not have faith in the estimates on which their schedules were based.

The further the job progressed the more woolly and guess-based the estimates were shown to be. The golf principle had not been recognised and certainly not utilised. Each project had in effect, been estimated on the assumption that a 'hole-in-one' would be achieved and that the whole course could be completed in eighteen strokes. However, the 'players' did not even know the length of the fairways...

... let alone the layout of the course...

PRACTICE - EXPERIENCE - CONVERGENCE

Although the answer to the problem was quite obvious, the implementation of the solution involved many changes to the company's marketing practices. Clients had to be convinced that a fixed-price for their computer system could not be arrived at until the project had progressed well beyond its early stages. They had to be educated to accept a provisional estimate for the entire system, with a firm fixed-price initially only applicable to its first or earliest one or two stages.

If for example, the project could be broken down into say, five stages, such as outline systems specification, systems design, program specification, coding and testing, followed by implementation, then a definite fixed-price would only be quoted for the first stage. The other four stages would therefore only be estimated on a strictly provisional basis.

Once the first stage had been completed, enough information and experience of that particular problem would have been gained to provide an accurate estimate for the next stage to be calculated.

More accurate revised estimates could then also be made for the third fourth and fifth stages, again based on the greater knowledge and experience gained through having now completed the first one.

It is a process of practice, experience and convergence - identical in principle to the game of golf. Utilising the increasing opportunity for accuracy as each shot in the direction of the target is completed.

A similar review and revision would of course take place at the end of the second stage, amending and consolidating the estimate and the price for the third stage, and again re-estimating the forth and fifth. The process rolled onwards at the completion of each stage.

This system was an immediate success, particularly with the team responsible for its actual systems design and software development. Each analyst and programmer gradually began to believe more in his or herself, in their knowledge, skills, and ability. Negative attitudes changed into positive ones. Individuals began to believe that those running the company finally understood what they did.

With the project teams no longer subject to the bullying and intimidation of a panicky management steadily losing its nerve as project after project lost money as the company moved towards insolvency, it was not surprising that morale improved and everyone began to believe that the tasks set them were fair and achievable targets.

Having at last been given realistic, achievable targets, the analysts and programmers began to complete modules ahead of schedule and below their cost budgets. Morale soared. Bonuses could at last be claimed. The revised estimating procedures were proving much more accurate. Everyone felt more involved with his or her projects. The teams believed they could complete even major tasks on time.

Work was now being done profitably and the company's fortunes were gradually being turned around. The only 'losers' were the sales team who had to develop a completely new approach, convincing clients that their very complex software development requirements could not be accurately estimated at the concept stage.

Some clients were lost. Mainly those unrealistic as to the cost of doing a good job or unconvinced of the problems involved, or those who simply believed in playing the market just to get the lowest price, irrespective of the quality problems it would bring. By and large these were all clients we really could do without. Our future lay with those who understood the complexity of the projects and could afford the time and expense to work in partnership with us to achieve the best result.

REALISTIC TARGETS

The importance of this anecdote is not to illustrate an insight on project management, but more to highlight the penalties of a common fault of bad leadership…
… the setting of 'impossible' targets…

The teams in the example had not been inherently incompetent but merely the victims of an unworkable policy. The instigators of that policy for its failure then blamed them. Eventually they began to believe it really was their fault. Not being in a position to themselves develop a solution through being in perpetual crisis-solving mode, inevitably they had lost their confidence and motivation.

TARGETS MUST BE BELIEVABLE

Targets must be seen to be attainable. That is an immutable rule of leadership. A person or a team required to achieve a target must confidently believe they stand a very good chance of meeting it. Establishing too difficult a goal will erode both the self-belief and self-confidence of those carrying out the task. No one enjoys being in a losing side. Doing so usually results in an actual reduction in the effort expended.

People sometimes understandably give up if they feel they have absolutely no chance of winning. The task then becomes even less achievable, the target even more elusive, often causing for all practical purposes the abandonment of maximum effort and relaxation into a slow comfortable pace.

KEEP THE TEAM FOCUSED

The self-confidence and job satisfaction of the team members must be maintained at all times. Therefore when a target has to be set that is either too remote or too complex to be reached comfortably in a single stage then interim targets or stages must be defined that can more realistically be achieved.

You should apply the same principles to your self. Never be too rigid in defining your ultimate objectives. Always have plenty of clearly defined more tangible ones along the way.

We all need regular success - make sure you are always within reach of a success or two. Make sure the same applies to the rest of your team. Remember perfection is seldom achievable - set yourself enough realistic targets to be always looking forward to shortly reaching the next one.

EMERGING AND CHANGING

Just as the perfect round of golf will probably never be achieved, then neither will the perfect career. The objective you start off with may be so remote that many of the stages towards its achievement are of necessity hazy. We are all individuals and circumstances beyond our control are forever emerging and changing. It is therefore likely that we will be able to see clearly only two or three career moves ahead.

You should also be an opportunist and be prepared to deviate from a career plan that is maybe too rigid, as circumstances change and more favourable conditions present themselves. Appreciate that we, as individuals also change.

The ambitions of youth are seldom the aspirations of middle age. Be prepared for a degree of flexibility. There are however many things we can do to improve our chances of success. Mostly, like the golf principle itself, they are common sense.

There is very little that is particularly new or clever in getting to the top. It is not necessary to excel in any of the traditional disciplines such as marketing, finance, human resources, or production. Neither is it necessary to have academic qualifications, although they can help open doors in the early days.

Many of our most successful entrepreneurs have little or no advanced education. Often this lack of qualifications, education, or a 'good background', acts as a spur, an incentive a source of motivation to scale great heights of achievement. Our commercial and industrial world is full of such examples.

Often it is far better if you are not a specialist in any of the traditional business disciplines as they can infect you with a form of tunnel vision, restricting the open-minded and balanced viewpoint essential to becoming a successful leader. The most important factors are character ones not qualifications... ... they are what we shall now explore...

KNOWING YOUR STRENGTHS

Everyone is good at something. I have said it before and will probably repeat it again. One of my own strengths is that I never readily write off anyone as being useless to an organisation. Wherever possible I try very hard to steer them into a position where they are making an effective contribution. If this is undertaken with due sensitivity to the individual and to his or her colleagues, it will have a positive and beneficial effect all round.

Obviously there are some who refuse to accept that they are not ideally suited to the slot they prefer, and it may be that the effort required to convince them otherwise could be better spent in other areas. Clearly not all situations have the potential for this exercise to be carried out.

Many sensible people are happy to remain in jobs that they do well, often declining a chance of promotion because it would be to a position that they feel would provide them with less job satisfaction. Aware of what they are contributing to the efficiency of their organisation, their competence bringing them the respect of their colleagues, they opt out of the promotion race preferring to stay in the job they are good at...
... such people tend to sleep well at nights...

Many others aim far too high, consequently living miserable lives full of excuses for their perceived •failure' to occupy a top job. Inevitably they blame others, or claim they are victims of the 'system'. Such people seldom criticise themselves or attempt to judge how their own misunderstanding and mishandling of their own strengths and weaknesses contribute to their career disappointments.

Although this book is primarily about leading others, successful leadership can only be accomplished from a base of understanding your own capabilities. Everyone falls very short of perfection in absolute terms, and also when compared against the characteristics of my ideal leader portrayed in Chapter One.

Like those you aspire to lead, you too are an individual unique in your combination of talents, emotions and other features. Just as you need to recognise and develop differing talents in others, you must first work on yourself.

SELF-ESTEEM

What is the most notable thing about you? What do you feel you have achieved most in your life so far? If you died today - what would you like written as your obituary or your epitaph?

Consider the following - if just one hundred people were to be preserved to perpetuate the human race, perhaps to colonise the Universe, and if it became compulsory to apply to join them. What would you claim as your qualifications to be one of that elite? What characteristics would you claim to be worthy of selection?

Any?

If you find this question difficult to answer convincingly, then you really need to work on improving your self-esteem. If it is merely modesty which precludes you from thinking you are in any way worth preserving, then that alone is a handicap because if you do not first and foremost believe in yourself you will find it difficult to get others to follow you.

It is not that you are undeserving of an obituary, not that you do not possess worthwhile qualifications to represent the human race. You maybe have just not got around to recognising them yet. There is nothing very alarming about this. It shows you perhaps have a little more thinking to do than you realised before you began reading this book.

Probably you are by now asking yourself, how does the author measure up to his own questions? I have anticipated this. My answer is: "I showed many others how to believe in themselves". Luckily I have achieved many things that I am proud of. Mostly they involved leading a team without which little would have been accomplished. My successes usually depended on having a successful team. Together we tackled many new and original problem areas, explored much 'unknown territory', produced a host of new answers and techniques.

I was very aware of the catalytic effect I had on my team but the bulk of the effort was theirs. Many of my protégés went on to very senior positions in other organisations and several now own their own very successful companies…
… we also had a lot of fun…

HOW HIGH?

However you have much to offer. You know that. We will now consider some of the characteristics in your personal make up. You must be realistic. If you are not totally realistic there is not much point in continuing this exercise.

In persevering this far it is likely that you are at least quite ambitious. What you need to recognise is the extent of your ambitions. Are you hoping to run the country, a local council, a large or a small company, a department of some institution, or least a small team?

Do you see yourself setting up your own organisation, or climbing up through the ranks of an existing one? Perhaps you do not know yet. Perhaps you just have an overriding sense that you are destined for some leadership role, that you can and will accomplish major successes. You may not be sure in what exact area this will be. This is perhaps the best state of mind in which to proceed, as too focused an ambition can blind you to opportunities as yet not encountered or identified.

Be sceptical about those who say they had a clear and single-minded vision and a sense of destiny from an early age. Very often the appetite for success and the driving force towards it has always existed but the absolute vision has been obscure. What is important is that the various opportunities are grasped en-route.

History is often re-written to portray someone as possessing from their earliest formative years, a single-minded and burning desire to reach some specific high office. It makes good reading often furnishing the popular media with good copy. Like many of our modern myths it is seldom reflected in real life. It has usually been embroidered or enhanced, just a part of the legend being established.

COURAGE

Are you courageous? Do you have 'guts'? You will not get anywhere if you do not have the stomach for a fight. As soon as your ambition starts to show, then some others will resent it. Even if you succeed in concealing how ambitious you really are there will be others who, either due to their own insecurity or to a paranoid suspicion of real or perceived rivals, will mark you down as ambitious, as competition to them, or just potentially dangerous.

Such people can be very treacherous, negative influences eroding the reputations of others, attempting to hold them back or even harass them into making mistakes or quitting the organisation. They may be genuine, formidable rivals to your ambitions, or merely 'dog in the manger' fashion trying to frustrate the hopes of more successful individuals, preventing them attaining the successes they themselves covert but do not have the abilities to attain.

REAL RIVALS

You will need to deal with such negative and destructive attitudes as a matter of routine. Be thick-skinned about these encounters. Far more courage will be needed to counteract the more serious ammunition of the more able, talented and ruthless of your rivals.

Some will seek to intimidate, discredit, humiliate, subvert, defame, set you up for failure, and generally damage your career. The difference will be that they will bring some of their corporate political skill to bear on you, the 'problem'.

Make no mistake you will need much courage to succeed. You are not very likely to climb rapidly and successfully for any length of time without making enemies. Once you reach the top it can be a very lonely place indeed, despite the numbers seeking your ear and your counsel.

Do not confuse physical courage, with the mental variety needed to further your career. It can be a very different commodity. For many years a close friend of mine displayed quite spectacular bravery whilst piloting advanced aerobatic aircraft, often performing manoeuvres far too violent and frequently much too close to the ground for my personal taste or stomach. Eventually he paid the ultimate penalty for his bravado, in a messy and purposeless contact with the ground. However throughout his business career, he had many times drawn back from situations that might bring him into serious confrontation or conflict with his boss. These were situations where I thought such confrontation to be professionally the right action…
… and morally justified…

By displaying more courage and using political skills to avoid these potential encounters, he would without doubt have advanced his career, and he knew it. He was, quite frankly, scared of confrontational corporate politics. Scared of initiating any political battle in case he lost and perhaps paid for it with his job.

In an aerobatic aircraft he had the courage of a lion. At work he was a wimp. He never lost his job or even a promotion opportunity through pushing too hard, even in situations where he clearly held all the cards. He never reached his full career potential either.

In the end what kept him from living to enjoy his treasured pension, was paradoxically not mental cowardice but his disdain for physical fear. If some of his physical courage had been transferred to his working day, and some of his business caution incorporated into his flying, he would probably be alive and running a major corporation today.
I regret that in the many hours we once spent contrasting this apparent contradiction in his personal make up, that I had not been more successful in persuading him to reverse his priorities.

SO, ARE YOU A WINNER?

It is fashionable to casually label other as 'winners' or 'losers'. These titles slip all too easily off many tongues without much thought being given to either justification or accuracy.

What do we mean by a winner? What do we mean by a loser? Who names the race or the competition the term applies to? What category do you think you are in? You will almost certainly claim but might not necessarily believe, that you are a winner. Most people, particularly those who aim for the top, would not admit to anything else. If you, hand on heart, are convinced one hundred percent that you are a winner, that you cannot fail…
… and then you probably would not be reading this book…

AVOID LOSERS

Assuming you are not a charity or a social worker - avoid where possible association with failure - it is contagious like an illness and similarly it takes time to recover from it.

SURVIVOR

If you think you know it all, then I probably have nothing more to say that will interest you. If so I am surprised I have retained your attention so far! If you suspect you may fall into the loser category, please do not give up now. You will 'lose' nothing by continuing. If you learn just one more useful thing, or even just understand or reinforce only one more important attribute, then you will finish further ahead than where you started off. A step in the right direction, progress on the winning trail. If you really are a loser…
… you have nowhere to go but to get better…

It could be of course that you would not choose to classify yourself in either the winner or the loser category. You might feel it is too early to tell. The chances are you regard yourself as a 'survivor'. If so, we are very much in business! Survival instincts are the strongest of all those we have, the most basic overriding all the others and dominating most aspects of behaviour in all living creatures.

The urge to win, to lead, to hold power - all stems from the basic survival instinct - arising from the subconscious desire to be as much in control of one's own destiny as possible, we try to arrange as many factors as we can that will improve our survival prospects. Affluence and power are perceived as contributing in this respect.

If you are a successful 'survivor' aided by your self-confidence and your courage, you can go forward and develop all your other talents and abilities.

INTELLIGENCE - INTUITION - INSTINCTS

Far too many people still confuse intelligence with the ability to attain academic qualifications. How many times have you heard the claim; "He must be intelligent, he's got a university degree"?

It is a sign of stupidity to confuse memory and learning ability with our basic animal intelligence, intuitive perception and reasoning, creativity and essential common sense. I prefer to consider 'intelligence' as a combination of many factors.

Firstly there is the raw Intelligence Quotient, the attempt to measure skills of perception, reasoning, and speed of thought without any contamination by training or any learned information.

Raw IQ on its own is a wasted resource. To be useful it has to be supported by an imagination powerful enough to create opportunities for its utilisation, otherwise strong logical and reasoning powers find expression in destructive, negative ways. It is always much easier to see the absurdities of a situation, the illogical nature of a position, the weak point in an argument, than to identify and construct a clear logical alternative.

LATERAL THINKING

The much-acclaimed gift of lateral thinking has its place too. More talked about than actually practised, the useful exponents of true lateral thinking are rare. However its usefulness is boundless, and apart from its direct benefit to the problem in hand, it arouses the admiration of others at all levels and creates a useful reputation for its originator.

Many other individual skills make up the package of 'intelligence' that we need on our way to the top. Included on the list must be a deep sense of curiosity about the world and the people around us, coupled with the perception to quickly understand why things are unravelling in such a way. The understanding of why a particular behaviour pattern has become established etc.

Do not overlook raw analytical ability either. There will be situations where such a talent will enable you to assess a situation with a speed and accuracy that will give you an advantage over your competitors.

Creativity has a very wide definition, as it is subject to so many specialisations. If you do not have it you may find it useful to have access to someone who does, as in our marketing oriented world ideas are an essential although a common commodity.

In most of today's leadership situations it is extremely useful to be able to think quickly and positively 'on your feet'. It is not always possible to avoid having to make an almost instant decision in a crisis, and those who are led invariably expect a fast intelligent response from their leaders.

SOMETHING WE JUST KNOW

In addition to the above I identify in every single person some degree of perhaps the most singularly useful talent required in the package of assets that make up the best leaders...

… it is best classified as instinct or intuition…

At its finest level it is an almost uncanny ability to 'know' the answer to a question, a problem, or to understand the implications of a situation, without benefit of any relevant advance knowledge, information or training…
… in fact a sixth sense…

Many people who hunt or fish exhibit this sixth sense to a remarkably high degree. Often it can be wholly or partly explained in such a context by a subconscious assimilation of many tiny clues, all-adding up to a likely happening or event that might lead to a success.

Even when the explanation is so simply it is still a powerful asset, and has often meant the difference between a good meal and an empty stomach. Such a sixth sense, whether a subconscious analysis, something more mysterious, or maybe a subtle combination of the two, is in no way restricted to hunting, fishing or related activities. It has surfaced with great frequency in genuine life or death survival situations, and is well known to many who have developed specialist skills to a high order.

It can and does exist in a work situation, alerting one to possible danger and acutely focusing attention to situations and opportunities.

EVERYONE HAS SOME

Everyone has this ability to some extent, but in a lucky few it has evolved (or maybe for them, never been lost), to a very high degree. Almost certainly a remnant from our distant ancestry when our senses were much more finely tuned to meet the needs of a hunter/gatherer society such instincts are still to be observed amongst bushmen and rainforest Indians, in the few areas where 'progress' has left them relatively untouched.

Where living is hard and survival is the norm, the strong survive and the weak perish. The top rungs of business can be very similar so it should not be surprising that some surviving 'primitive' instincts and skills come back into good use in the leadership arena.

Interestingly often the 'better educated' and 'more highly qualified' amongst us seem to retain less of these ancient skills. You have only to look at the many who have built significant business empires from humble beginnings to understand the value of an uncluttered and open mind coupled with the hungry, aggressive instincts of the natural predator. I find no problem in detecting certain logic in that.

If you have the instincts and abilities to which I refer, then you will have already understood what I mean. You will also possess a gift that will prove immeasurably helpful in two-way communication with others and in rapidly assessing a situation almost as if it were by some kind of osmosis or telepathy. Used intelligently it can work for you in so many ways and enable you to help others give of their best.

NEGOTIATION - COMMUNICATION - DELEGATION

All the above skills will be required in a leader's repertoire - if you already have them all in some form or other, then so much the better. However they can often be developed to some extent as required, the most important ingredient being our old friend 'common sense'. It is also important to have some diplomatic skills, obvious vital components in negotiation, delegation, motivation and communication activities.

PERSONALITY AND STYLE

So you naturally attract attention without trying to do so? Are others immediately aware of your presence when you enter a room? So you in fact have 'presence'? How much does your appearance and style make a statement about you?

It is not necessary to drive around in a Ferrari or to wear silk suits to make an impact. Going to the other extreme in dress and possessions may also make a big impression but it might not be the desired one. Some people just seem to have a natural presence. If this applies to you, then again you have a very valuable asset - one, which can be developed and utilised.

Would you describe yourself as assertive or as aggressive? Assertiveness is currently a fashionable characteristic that many enrol on courses to learn. Like so many other useful leadership skills, if you have to go on a course in an attempt to acquire it you probably do not have enough of the natural commodity to play in the first division. Aggression, although not fashionable like assertiveness, should not be overlooked. Aggression can, when used in a controlled and constructive manner, save a great deal of time when compared with gentler more 'acceptable' techniques.

Natural self-confidence is of course, one of our important assets, indeed a key one instrumental to the most effective deployment of the others. It is often very difficult to judge whether someone is genuinely self-confident or merely putting on a very convincing act.

It does not matter either way as long as the result has the desired effect. Many apparently self-confident individuals are merely playing out a role albeit in a totally convincing manner. Mostly they did not start off in that way but became aware of the desirability of the self-confidence and work very hard at projecting it.

Often the acting grows into the genuine article, the role-playing changing into real confidence, heuristic learning process turning into evolution of a genuine characteristic. Thus self-confidence can be developed, it is just that we all start from a different base line. Sooner or later however, anyone can develop the real thing. If you learn to convince others that you are self-confident, to all intents and purposes you will eventually become so.

ENDLESS NEEDS

We could continue ad infinitum exploring the skills, talents, personality characteristics and other factors, some of them essential, others quite useful in developing effective leadership ability.

Most people respond best to an honest open style of communication. They like fairness and they respond to plain speaking. Ideas, suggestions and problems are expected to be given a fair hearing. Sensible employees do not expect their boss to be perfect; we would have even more industrial discontent if such were demanded. Respect will invariably be shown to those who admit their mistakes, in sharp contrast to the ones who try to maintain a myth of their own infallibility.

DECISIVENESS

Working for someone who has difficulty making decisions or who takes a lengthy time to do so is a most frustrating experience. Often there seems very little point in the senior slot being occupied if the incumbent is indecisive. Yet such bosses predominate. Normally it is fear that inhibits the decision-making process - the fear of making the wrong decision. Yet it should be obvious that no one will make the correct decisions all the time.

Indecisive individuals have no right to be leaders. Good leadership is all about decision-making. It is what leaders are paid to do. If they do not need to make decisions, then is their job really necessary? I cannot respect indecisive people who are in charge of others. Do you? How decisive are you? Have you ever taken responsibility for any really major decisions in your work?

HARD WORK

A willingness to work hard coupled with an appreciation of the dedicated efforts of others. Knowing how to express gratitude - capable of graciously thanking others for their efforts and not seeming to patronise them. Give appropriate rewards for your team, well thought out and stimulating incentives... ... all these have their place...

Will you always put your team first? Will you fight tooth and nail for them? Will you assume responsibility even when they have been wrong? How sensitive are you to their life-styles, their backgrounds, history, family circumstances and financial problems? Do you overcome your own occasional bouts of boredom and frustration in the interests of motivating others and maintaining their high level of enthusiasm?

Do you have a record of picking winners as far as staff is concerned? Do you understand how and why you form opinions regarding others? Building and maintaining a team is very much about picking winners, a winning team, and guiding and helping their development.

INSECURITY

Many of those in senior positions in our commercial and industrial life have a significant fear of rivalry from their subordinates, and consequently often discriminate in favour of less able individuals when promoting and recruiting.

It is a confident, assured and well-balanced person who will recruit or promote a potential rival. However, if you think carefully, they are the very ones who should be selected to ensure the very strongest possible team is assembled and maintained.

Most of us naturally feel this insecurity. Surprisingly to some observers the very best leaders use such insecurity constructively, selecting the most able and talented, accepting the pressure they themselves may come under from them, but understanding that it will force them, despite being in charge, to perform even better in order to justify remaining at the top.

WANTING IT IS NOT ENOUGH

Are you flexible? Do you want to bring change into your organisation? Do you want to transform it in some way or re-organise it. Maybe change its products or marketing direction?

If you start the process of change can you direct it, can you control it, successfully identifying each subtle deviation from the optimum path, then steering things back on track?

Do you have the skills, sensitivity and diplomacy to control the emotions, and the conflicts that would be unleashed?

Wanting to be the boss is not enough. Just wanting status, money and power, never achieved it. You must have the potential, the talents and skills the conviction enthusiasm and the courage. Merely wanting is not enough. It's up to you!

KEY POINTS

*   A round in eighteen - the ultimate objective
*   Unrealistic targets break spirits
*   Frequent and regular success is vital - reward each step
*   Lack of education - often a positive motivation in later life
*   Traditional business disciplines often cause tunnel vision
*   Everyone is good at something - sensitive leaders identify and develop it in others
*   To understand hopes and fears of others - first know your own
*   Courageous and thick-skinned - only way to fight for your team
*   Winner - loser - or survivor?
*   Sixth sense is less well educated
*   Natural presence and self-confidence - an art to learn -a gift to use
*   Indecisive leaders - contradiction in terms
*   Insecure, frightened bosses pick weak teams - they do not lead
*   Wanting is not enough

Lack of education - often-positive self-motivation much had been covered in this chapter. All of it is relevant to our objective of being effective leaders. Subsequent chapters will explore how you leadership potential can be developed to become more effective in the most vital areas.

FOUR
On The Way Up

Unless you are one of those rare exceptionally gifted individuals, seemingly destined for the top without having to work particularly hard at getting there, then the earlier you start to plan, practice and sharpen your leadership skills the better.

Most people need and indeed want to be led, even if they refuse to acknowledge it other than on a subconscious level. You can see the evidence of this everywhere, from the common reluctance to use initiative or the unwillingness to take responsibility that is encountered in every sphere of our working lives.

We also live in a society that increasingly seeks to relieve us of individual accountability for many aspects of our very existence. In areas such as education, health-care, housing, pensions, our freedom to choose for is restricted unless an individual is financially strong enough to stay outside the system.

There exists an increasing devolution to bureaucratic bodies of those responsibilities that often would be best undertaken by individuals themselves. The aptly named 'nanny state' has affected an insidious erosion of the concept of personal responsibility. In this age a typical response to most problems is 'why doesn't someone do something about it?' The 'someone' is the state, the local council, and the police, perhaps the fire brigade. Anyone in fact except the individuals themselves.

All this just adds power to the hands of the bureaucrats, that most un-stimulating and inefficient form of management (I cannot bring myself to call it leadership), thriving as they do on the reluctance or inability of others to cope for themselves. Bureaucrats thrive on the dependency of others on the 'system'.

EVERYONE NEEDS LEADERSHIP

However although almost all of the population needs leadership they show a marked reluctance to seeing others from their peer group aspire to the position. I learned this lesson at a very early age. As a child belonging to a extremely poor family I was lucky enough to pass the eleven-plus examination, consequently gaining a place at the local grammar school.

Such a seemingly innocent step towards improving my future prospects was far from welcome by the other local families in our socio-economic group, a small Norfolk farming community. It caused alienation. I had suddenly become different. Rare in our village for someone of my background to attend grammar school, I was perceived as seeking, rather too successfully, to climb out of the level of squalor and poverty we lived in. It was to me an important early lesson that I have remembered throughout my life.

POLARISED ATTITUDES

Among the micro society encapsulated in our little village talent with one's fists was acceptable acclaimed and indeed encouraged. Brainpower was not. Many accused me of seeing myself as 'better' than the other kids I mixed with...
...true, I thought I was...

Physically I was just as tough as the others. I could run further and faster than most. I could climb, fish, hunt, and do all the things we did, just as well and in most cases better than the rest of them.

In addition I knew I was much brighter, more creative, and possessed a much higher level of initiative. No wonder I triggered off some alienation in such a close and inward looking community, particularly in those days before the electronics age had broadened the general outlook on the world, and migration from the larger cities had diluted the inbred attitudes of Norfolk farming communities.

It became a situation that I rapidly had to learn to handle and control else my life would have been made unbearable. It was one of the first major steps I consciously took towards developing the skills of leading others. Previously I had displayed certain natural leadership ability. Always followed by my 'gang' a group of boys, many of them older than me, who would do my bidding.

Being quite good with my fists, and at the time possessed of a very aggressive nature, physical intimidation had served me well in lieu of more refined 'management techniques'. Such methods served me very well until the age of eleven or so. After that the resentment caused by my attendance at grammar school necessitated several changes to the methods I used, both to hold my gang together and to lead them effectively.

GROWING AWARENESS

I became more acutely aware of my natural advantages in the IQ department but much more importantly I grew more conscious of the need to apply basic psychology as a leadership tool. As we grew older the other boys gravitated towards agricultural work initially part-time at first during the summer holidays, exercising their muscles if not their minds but eventually giving some of them a physical edge over me.

No longer could I be confident of battering a laggard or dissenter back into line. It became much more urgent to apply or to concentrate on subtle persuasion, guile and reasoning. Forced to improve my communication skills (more mouth - less fists), I started concentrating my understanding on what best motivated the others.

Needing to overcome their resentment of my alleged ambitions and their belief that I desired to eventually get away from the village and escape the poverty we all were experiencing, I had to continually convince them in ever more original ways that they still needed me. Looking back it was a very formative experience.

DEPARTING THE LAND OF RIVERS

Later, after quitting school and finding work in London, I decided to sever contact with my village roots. It was in some ways a painful decision. I found myself unable to reconcile the growing conflict between my emerging adult ambitions and the calls and demands remaining from my childhood village life. The gap was far wider than merely geographical, the one hundred and twenty miles between sleepy central Norfolk and the fleshpots of the capital. To a somewhat naive sixteen year old, it was a whole different world…
… a massive culture shock…

With my unsophisticated farm labouring ways, speaking loudly in the broadest of 'Naarrfuk' accents, I might just well have gone around with a straw in my mouth or have even arrived from the planet Mars. I seemed to be an alien.

Confused, often out of my depth, in the big city, I made a painful but conscious decision. I literally and metaphorically turned my back on the place of my birth and worked on a new image. I needed to almost construct a new identity, from a gauche teenager uncertain and insecure, looking for work and a new life in the metropolis. I seldom returned to Norfolk, growing apart and distant from the people and things that had been familiar.

Only in recent years have I seriously attempted to go back. Too late, the things of greatest value are no longer there. 'Progress' has seen to that. It was in retrospect a very painful and character forming period, and one about which I still, so many years after, retain some regrets.

ALL HAVE TO START SOMEWHERE

I am assuming you are good, or at least competent at what you do professionally. This book is not about being a good salesman, accountant, or computer programmer. Many other works cover these topics comprehensively. Let us assume that you are at least average, or better than average in your specialised subject although not necessarily brilliant at it.

You probably have not yet arrived at the top, or if so are showing some of the thoroughness that got you there by reading this and not leaving anything to chance. Probably you are not merely ambitious, but believe passionately in possessing the ability to run the show. You probably feel your talents lie not only in your specialised profession, but also in a chief executive role or other top job.

Probably like me, you have a history of exercising some form of leadership, possibly dating from your childhood or late teens. You want to be the one in charge perhaps of your present department or division or maybe the entire company. It is unlikely, as you already know well, that you will leap from the very bottom to the very top in one straightforward bound. So what can you do to prepare the way? How can you gently exercise and train those skills vital to your ambition? How may you hone and expand these talents on the way up without provoking an undue amount of counter productive alienation?

We will assume that you expect to rise through the various levels towards your ultimate goal, spending only the minimum time at each stage necessary to acquire the experience you need to affect an impact.

Perhaps you make some strategic job changes, joining new employers as part of your overall career plan. Moves made purely for financial gain should be discounted as they invariably run counter to any ruthless leadership ambition, although many claim otherwise.

DECIDING ON AN IMAGE

By the time you have reached the top job you will almost certainly have your own identifiable image, probably a mixture of fact, myth, and reputation plus much embroidery and enhancement added by others to portray you the way they would like to see you.

Possibly you will be depicted as 'larger than life' in some respects. Certainly any tendency towards even mild eccentricity will be exaggerated, as will interesting aspects of your appearance, habits, lifestyle or working methods. You are likely to acquire certain 'trade marks' identifying you as different. Do not let this process alarm or upset you in any way. Instead turn them to your advantage.

Often success is helped or speeded up by being noticed. However conceal or at least tone down anything that could be used against you on the way up. Allow others to notice only the positive differences, those contributing positively to your image. When you have reached the top you can get away with what many would classify as a high degree of eccentricity but whilst you are still lower down in the pecking order it is a mistake to be noted for an image departing too far from the norm. Be different but not too different.

If you are at heart a maverick, do not rush to show it. The world has a great need for those who reject convention and determinedly prove their individual way is right, but others can be slow to accept new ideas and often even slower to accept those who set out to promote them without care or concern for their colleagues. Play your 'hands' cautiously at least until you have a complete understanding of the minds and the motivations of those around you.

LIFE OUTSIDE THE OFFICE

By all means be known for your sartorial elegance or for some exceptional sporting achievement, artistic accomplishment or exciting leisure pursuit. Often these activities will attract interest and generally favourable comment and gossip.

Beware of making interests known which will attract jealousy, adverse gossip, or even worse, scandal. Even owning a Ferrari, Porsche or inheriting a country estate whilst employed in a lowly paid job, will not endear others to your cause, particularly if they are in direct competition with you for promotion or a choice assignment. Similarly do not openly court or publicise social   relationships with influential or powerful members of the organisation who are very senior to you.

I once had a college who had been driven from his previous job due to an inheritance enabling him to buy a car far superior and expensive than that driven by his boss - no perhaps something that could be tolerated in today's world but the resentment would still be there.

Your ambitions would be signalled in a clumsy fashion, perceived as too far too fast, and label you as perhaps someone not to be trusted with information that others would not wish to be heard at the top. Not a good way to avoid unnecessary conflict.

Always strive to develop a natural form of leadership that involves promoting the interests of your colleagues as well as your own. Always be conscious that you are grooming and conditioning them into loyalty towards you when you eventually reach the top. Get them to gradually see for themselves the qualifications you have for the leadership role...
... aim for respect and not resentment...

POSSIBLE TO BE TOO SUCCESSFUL

There may be times when the best strategy is not to appear too talented and successful. Consider a new salesperson joining an established but only average performing small team of three or four others. If the newcomer is of exceptional ability does he or she immediately show it, even if the company desperately needs lots more sales? In reality by being too successful the new recruit could alienate the established team members and possibly cause their defection.

Although the successful newcomer might consider him or herself to be acting in the best interests of the company and merely performing at their natural high level, it is possible that such performance could be counter to the company's best interests. If, by unintentionally driving away some or all of the remaining three members of the sales team the total sales figures drop, then despite the considerable individual success the company might find itself in even greater trouble. The 'successful' newcomer would not be popular with the boss.

A good team leader would identify the potential for this if it exists and will take steps to avoid the problem. However if you are in a position analogous to that of my hypothetical salesperson, then you should not put the others in a position where resentment of your talents cause them to desert the team or for their performance to deteriorate.

There will always be ways or demonstrating your superiority without alienating everyone else. If you can accomplish this, at the same time subtly communicating your understanding of the ramifications relative to others in the team and your way of successfully solving it, then the benefits to you should be obvious.

BE AWARE OF YOUR FUTURE IMAGE

Deliberate development and tuning of an image that will serve you all the way to the top needs very careful planning and continual attention. You are creating something which right or wrong, could be with you for the rest of your life. You therefore have every incentive to get it right.

It is better to delay embarking on this aspect of your career development until you are sure of the direction in which you are focusing your image, than to risk creating the wrong one by an over-hasty premature launch. I still have anecdotes told about things I was reputed to have done more than twenty-five years ago, few of them, which are flattering.

The question of what image or what style to aim at is a very difficult one to decide upon. The best answer has to lie very much with you as an individual.

Obviously it would be foolish to attempt to build a reputation around things at which you do not excel, or which you cannot carry off with a certain amount of flair. It is a variation of the age-old advice of only entering the races in which you stand a good chance of winning.

The supposed virtue of taking part or just playing the game for the sporting sake of doing so is merely so much propaganda, designed to furnish an endless supply of losers in order to make the pundits look good...
... no one gets very far by losing...

Leaving aside for a moment the more human, personal side of your image, the main thrust of your planning should be towards attributes, perceived or real, crusades, reputed expertise or other fame, that can be directly channelled to your organisation's benefit.

Areas well worth considering are customer service, cost cutting, product enhancement, timesaving ideas, public relation stunts etc. Acquiring a reputation that you are continually striving for the company's success, but in a way that involves and enthuses colleagues can only begin to mark you out as potential promotion material.

Make sure however that you always try to apply rules of diplomacy and tact in both suggesting and working at your ideas and improvements. Do not do too much too quickly unless you are sure of convincing most of your team (including your boss) of its usefulness and viability.

Remember your peer group as well as your bosses will watch you. Be careful not to alienate them any more than absolutely necessary, and then only when you are so securely right that there can be no conceivable comebacks.

I am not a great fan of popularity, but many managers are. They may be reluctant to support, let alone promote someone who is unpopular with colleagues.

Try wherever possible to involve your direct colleagues in your ideas and schemes. Invite their comments and suggestions and allocate them fair credit when submitting your proposals. You will then, correctly gain their support and enthusiasm and the project will be far more likely to succeed. Your leadership ability will also be starting to make it felt in a natural and effective way.

CAREFULLY POLISH YOUR IMAGE

Work on your image. Do nothing too dramatic too quickly. Always be reasonably sure of your ground before making the next move. Remember you are building something that will stay with you for all your working life. Progress cautiously analysing the effect of everything you do.

As you rise nearer the top then your image can be expanded and enhanced in many ways. Indeed you will often be expected to display symbols of your success and to show signs of mild eccentricity in your dress, hairstyle, manner etc. It is important that success is seen to bring its rewards otherwise your team may not try so hard to get to the top themselves.

If you are too vigorous in hiding the rewards of your own success from your colleagues, then they might get the impression that you are embarrassed by those rewards, and therefore possibly you are not yourself truly convinced you deserve them.

When I was the Technical Director of a software house many years ago and poised to take over as Managing Director, I initially refused to accept the moderately expensive company car that came with the job. The company car I choose to drive was a rather battered high mileage Mini that has seen much better days. I loaned it to anyone in my team who needed a car during working hours and it was effectively used as a pool car, albeit one on which I had priority. The vehicle was always littered with punched cards, magnetic tapes and other computer paraphernalia (that dates the story). It seemed part of my image at that time, making a point out of not needing an expensive and pristine vehicle and bragging about how much my sacrifice was saving the company.

EXAMPLE?

I suppose I was hoping to set some sort of example and dampen down the constant pressure we were under to provide more and more staff with cars. As far as my own needs were concerned if I wanted to drive at 150 miles per hour, I personally owned a Gordon Keeble that more than catered for any of my latent boy-racer urges. Also I had recently taken to flying light aircraft as a hobby and was about to acquire a half-share in one. I therefore considered the fast sporty side of my image to be well taken care of in the way I wanted it to be.

Shortly afterwards the shareholders invited me to take over the managing director slot. However I choose to keep the old Mini as my company car, still thinking I was setting a good example. My mistake became apparent shortly afterwards when a delegation from my team complained to me about the vehicle.

It was not, so they claimed, that the MD's choice of an old mini would inhibit them from requesting more expensive cars for themselves. I surely knew them better than that.

Apparently it was the impression they judged it would make with our customers. What would they think if they saw our MD driving around in an old mini - particularly one that was freely used by all the staff who did not have a company vehicle of their own? Would the customers not think perhaps we were in severe financial trouble? What was I trying to do to the company image? Finally I conceded they might have a point. Relenting, we acquired a Lancia Zagato sports car for my use. My team approved, generally considering that it reflected the certain 'sporty' image they has come to expect of me…
… it was also fun for them to borrow…

FLYING THE FLAG

Moving on a few years, having expanded the software house into a small group of computer services companies, I became seriously interested in racing aircraft as my main leisure interest. Rather than resenting their chief executive's indulgence in this very expensive sport, my team asked me if they could in some way become involved in it.

Soon we had painted the company name and logo on the aircraft and I was training my sales director as unofficial co-pilot and navigator. It was an honour to discover colleagues of all levels from within the company turning up to support me at airfields all over the country.

Before long the sales team were inviting clients to the air races and providing hospitality facilities. They linked these activities with PR in the trade press. Far from resenting my 'extravagant' life-style they were involving themselves with it, and at the same time turning it to the company's advantage in sales and marketing. Obviously they were getting a lot of fun out of it as well. Furthermore it was their own ideas that led to participation and client involvement. I had been very careful not to suggest any such thing.

For a season or two we even flew a company racing team with two of my sales team racing against me. It was all good stuff for company morale.

Indeed it went even further. Several of my people became so interested in aviation that they themselves learned to fly becoming very enthusiastic pilots. One very enthusiastic and hard working programmer assigned to a project in the USA, worked so hard in his first three months there, it enabled him to buy a second-hand light aircraft out of his overtime earnings. Fortunately my fears that his productivity would then drop due to him spending too much time flying, proved unfounded.

I could all too easily have alienated my colleagues with my image and life-style of owning, flying and racing fast aircraft. However I made sure I involved them in every way possible. Anyone interested in aviation was taken for a flight and persuaded to take the controls to find out for themselves how easy it is to fly the things.

Those interested in obtaining a pilot licence were encouraged and introduced to the best instructors. Where priority, cost and time constraints were favourable my aircraft were used on company business, visits to distant clients, deliveries of urgently required equipment etc. We even used them as an efficient way of visiting computer exhibitions at the National Exhibition Centre, so conveniently located virtually on Birmingham airport. The whole exercise generated enthusiasm and heightened company morale.

UNDERSTANDING OTHERS

Unless you are an expert at understanding other people, you will never be really successful at leading them. We cannot all progress through life without possessing this ability to a greater or a lesser extent. Many holding this ability do not make use of it. Sometimes they do not recognise it, certainly many do not make a conscious effort to improve this skill. It can, apart from its obvious benefits in gathering information, also make life much more interesting for the observer. As a skill it is one that can be very much self-taught.

We are perhaps at our most perceptive in the very earliest years of our lives, learning from observation and imitation from the beginning of our days. Often we become lazy about this habit of observation, choosing to be very selective in what we see in others. It is therefore very important that we review our application of this important skill, if necessary training ourselves to be more effective in the way we observe and consequently understand our fellow humans. If we do not understand them we can never hope to lead them effectively.

How do we go about this? Again this is one of those areas where some people have a natural advantage over others. You will need to assess your own aptitude in this skill before making a judgement of the areas in which you need to improve. Like most things, no hard and fast rules exist that are relevant to each and every one of us.

Individuals always will have their own tried and valid techniques that would refute any rules I may try to impose. There are however some accepted and proven techniques that should make a good starting point from which to evolve your own style and methods.

DON'T 'LISTEN BUT NOT HEAR'

First and foremost be a good listener. I repeat this without apology. Sight and sound are our main ways of receiving information about others. Many people 'listen but do not hear'. It is easy to fall into this trap. Hours of listening to crushing bores at parties will soon cultivate this listening without hearing habit, making the correct social grunting noises at appropriate moments, signalling understanding and agreement, but all the while coasting along on autopilot.

We are all sometimes guilty of this but it is not a good habit to fall into despite being an easy one. Listening correctly can be hard work. Not everybody can present himself or herself in an interesting manner…
… everyone however has something interesting to say…

Learn to concentrate whilst listening. Think ahead to identify the next interesting question you are going to ask. Concentrate on formulating questions that will not merely act as polite dialogue but contribute to the conversation. Invite others to develop their subjects. Work hard at getting them to expand and elaborate.

You may be very surprised how interesting the most seemingly boring person can become. It is all too easy to stifle others by subconsciously communicating to them the fact that you find them less than stimulating. They then often give up trying to interest you.

Remember, every single person has interesting things to say. They all have hopes, fears, pride and aspirations, all of which are important to them and to those they work with if an effective team is to be built. Even the very fact that you appear to be finding them interesting can change the most seemingly boring or uninteresting person into someone who is a pleasure to talk with. Remember be interested in others...
... show them you are interested in them...

OTHER COMMUNICATION

I repeat, we rely heavily on vision as well as on sound for interpersonal communication. I do not intend to reproduce the many works already written about body language. Much of it is I believe vastly oversimplifies, and only of superficial interest because so many basic body language signals are now so widely understood that many use them deliberately to send a false message. It is a form of 'body language lie'.

It is also easy for the skilled practitioner of deliberate body language to use it to provoke an intended reaction from companions, an indication of its interactive nature. It becomes very simple to trigger in others certain reactions as they respond to your own signals. This can result in a kind of body language dialogue, which unless all the participants know the 'rules' can get very confusing and lead to some very inaccurate communication.

Some aspects of body language such as the spoken variety are not the unique natural signals often claimed but have differing interpretations in some countries and cultures. This can trigger some interesting and unplanned interpretation, especially in an international or multi-culture situation.

Body language is at its most useful when you are not consciously trying to communicate or interpret it. When conscious use of this media takes place in a group where some or all of those present consider themselves skilled to some degree in its deployment, we have a situation analogous to differing skills of speaking a foreign language, but with the important omission of not so easily recognising differing levels of competence.

It is perhaps best classified at the same level of usefulness as hand-writing analysis and psychometric testing, both of which I regard as discredited especially when used in a relatively casual context and not subjected to strictly controlled conditions and restrictions.

Many of the theories concerning body language, taught for example on sales training courses, are of very limited value. This applies especially to individuals already possessing considerable natural ability and who are probably already instinctively superior in the subject. However it would be wrong of me to dismiss the topic too casually.

It is unfortunate that such obsession with training courses has led to many people teaching themselves to convey deliberate body language signals with poor results, often conveying the 'message' in an exaggerated sometimes-comical manner. It is most useful to interpret body language from those sending them when off their guard. You then get natural accurate signals, and not ones they have programmed themselves to transmit.

SENSITIVITY

Be sensitive to the views and the feelings of others. A word or a comment that you might personally find harmless or in some circumstances even a compliment, can cause pain and resentment in others. If someone describes me as 'hard', meaning that I possess certain toughness or resilience, then I regard it as a compliment, irrespective of whether that was the intention. Many would however, be offended, feeling themselves thought of as insensitive or lacking in the caring department.

TOLERANCE

Always look beneath the surface when considering others. Most people hide their true feelings for much of the time, in case others gain an impression that is not intended. Often it is the fear of appearing vulnerable. Make a habit of always establishing eye-to-eye contact when communicating. Most individuals do not do this…
… particularly when outside their intimate circle of contacts…

71

The experienced practitioner of eye-to-eye contact is more able to detect evasion, acting, and the conveyance of inaccurate information by others. It also suggests that you are far more sincere than someone who avoids direct eye contact, obviously aiding you transmitting your message.

Always search beyond the obvious. By this I do not mean you should automatically mistrust those you deal with, more that you should practice looking deeper. An unusual or unexpected reaction from someone might be caused by circumstances unknown to you. They might have problems or concerns that they choose to hide. You must view such an occurrence as a signal to be sensitive and not put that person under unnecessary pressure.

Study your colleagues' habits and their working patterns. This will help you identify when they have a problem either at work or outside, perhaps one in which you can help them in some way. Be prepared to show your understanding of others by acting as their counsellor if they wish it. You can construct lasting bonds of loyalty this way.

The foundations of mutual loyalty paved by this process will often prove invaluable if the person you have understood, advised and helped, forms part of your team in the years to come.

If you find yourself, formally or informally, in a counselling role with a colleague, whatever happens never betray their confidence. To do so is an unforgivable sin. It would indicate to others that you are unfit for a leadership position, where respect and trust are of the utmost importance.

By betraying such a trust you would inevitably and justifiably lose respect, and probably would never again be confided in by those in the know. Not a good start when aspiring to lead others. Refrain also from gossip. Even if by gossiping you are not actually betraying a confidence, it could well appear to others as if you are.

OPINIONS

Never dismiss the opinions of others out of hand unless of course you deliberately intend to humiliate them. Several well-known international tycoons seem to have attended the 'school of management by intimidation and humiliation', but I would not recommend it as your policy, unless of course you have so much money you can afford to buy a form of 'loyalty' and have no need for respect, other than for your purchasing power.

Understand that everyone has reasons for holding a particular point of view. If that person has any importance to you, and most should have, then their views should be treated with respect however much you personally disagree with them. If they are not important to you in any way, then an out of hand dismissal of someone else's viewpoint is just plain old-fashioned bad manners…
… would you really intend that?

Where you feel it is important to get your own contradictory point across, consider alternatives to direct argument. Formulate questions designed to explore the opposing viewpoints. Design them to seek out enlightening detail, and to amplify and extend the meaning of the other person's views.

You may of course find yourself not as current in your own assumptions as you believed. Your views might therefore change in some way. There is little point in dogmatically sticking to a position if you are not right. Alternatively, if you are right, the reverse might occur. The other party might come to accept your opinion when encouraged to think more carefully through their own position. Your tactful probing questions should be subtly aimed at engineering just that.

Avoid unnecessary direct confrontation with other members of the team you are part of. Become known as a mediator, a diplomat. Acknowledged as someone who gets things to happen, a person who brings about progress? Not somebody who delays progress through confrontational petty point scoring.

By carefully developing your talents at understanding and interacting constructively with your immediate colleagues, you will practice and enhance skills that will prove priceless when you are in a top job. You will in addition help build the confidence of others, whilst of course reinforcing your own.

All this will project you more naturally into a leadership role, and ensure a high degree of loyalty and acceptance when your claim to that role is recognised.

MANAGING YOUR BOSS

We do not, if we are ambitious and intelligent, just manage or lead those who report to us. Leave aside the word 'lead' for a moment and consider the word 'manage'. My copy of the Pocket Oxford Dictionary defines the word 'manage' as; 'handle, wield, control, organise'.

To a greater or lesser extent we can, and at times find it useful to handle, wield, control or organise in some way, not just colleagues at our own level, but also our boss or bosses. This must obviously be a subtle and invisible process, particularly to the one who is being manipulated or managed, as it would almost certainly be interpreted as a weakness on their part for allowing it to take place.

In some common working relationships of course, this apparent reversal of the normal role, whereby the subordinate partner exercises some degree of organisational control over the boss is normal and accepted. An example of this obviously exists in many boss/secretary relationships where the secretary often exercises a considerable degree of control over the boss's schedule, and also who they are 'allowed' to meet in the normal course of the working week.

Often a powerful secretary will exert a sometimes-alarming amount of other influence particularly in personnel matters. There are many incidences, some of them in high political circles where close aides have probably changed the course of major events by their assumed power to 'control' access to the boss. One of the first things I learned when I started working in offices was 'chat up the secretary if you want to get to the boss'.

Such an obvious direct influence is not what I am discussing here. More the situation where a subordinate builds up a relationship with the boss through either a mentor/protégé one, or just through good communication, and can achieve influence, manipulation and indeed power well in excess of that normally available to someone of their status within the organisation.

Often we may find it desirable to persuade our boss to change habits in some way, or to adopt a new style or practice that will make our lives easier or add to general efficiency. Into this category comes the secretary training the boss to call the office more frequently for messages whilst away on business, or nagging him or her into using the personal computer he has been so reluctant to tackle.

More importantly we may also persuade the boss to regularly visit and personally review our section of the operation thereby increasing team morale and improving efficiency, at the same time giving exposure to our own, hopefully successful endeavours. A closer insight into how we run things, and an opportunity to promote pet ideas and schemes.

FLAWS

We all have weaknesses in our characters. One of the most common ones in those who achieve the top positions is a necessity to have an audience for all their accomplishments. For activities which are of obvious merit and likely to meet with widespread approval this proves no problem. Such events are readily made public. I refer more specifically to those events in the realm of corporate politics that often, by their very nature, have to be devious and secret.

In the jungle of the boardroom and the top echelons within many organisations, many deeds are simply not fit for public consumption, or at least their perpetrators do not consider them so. However those who pull such strokes invariably need someone else to witness, acknowledge and applaud their cleverness.

The victim is seldom in a position to know how the deed was done and anyway would probably not show much appreciation, let alone publicise how they had been out-manoeuvred.

Clever, manipulative, politically inclined individuals more often than not have this flaw of needing an audience when they think they are being exceptionally devious or excelling in some activity which some might consider underhand. They then need their audience, one it can trust with the confidentiality of their deed.

If you identify this character flaw in your boss, then look for an opportunity to show in some discrete and subtle way, your admiration and appreciation of his or her talents. You are then very likely to be recognised as one who understands and admires not just the cleverness that has been employed, but also the need for devious and ruthless behaviour which others might find disturbing - this will likely lead to your selection as the 'audience' to similar future deeds.

A bond will then arise between you and your boss, which if you handle tactfully and skilfully could serve you well in many ways. On no account seek to use the information so acquired by sharing it with a third party. Resist any inclination to arrange your own audience for what is in reality your own growing involvement in the corporate political arena. You do not have to copy the mistakes of others…
… instead, learn from them…

WATCH, WAIT, LISTEN AND LEARN

Utilise such a confidential relationship with your boss as a medium to communicate your own ideas and suggestions with the timing controlled by you. Never attempt to convert the sensitive information you hear into ammunition. Doing so would only spawn a powerful adversary. One, which could destroy, not further your ambitions. Avoid if possible, getting

too involved in the politics. Watch, wait, and show admiration if you really mean it...
... watch, wait and learn...

You must of course resolve that when you reach the top, never to show similar weaknesses.

FRIENDS

Although most of us take pleasure from the company of their friends, and enjoy exchanging advice with them, their presence in a working environment can complicate events considerably. A high degree of social contact is usually necessary with both colleagues and other business acquaintances.

In helping to construct the bonds essential for successful teamwork, these bonds also lubricate the trading wheels that assist so much in the generation of business. However I refuse to classify such relationships as friendship although that over-used word is so often spoken in that context. It is perhaps a matter of definition.

The term 'friend' is one of the most over-worked words in the English language. Inevitably it has become devalued by being used so often as a substitute for acquaintance, comrade, pal, or companion. Unfortunately it is such a convenient word. In the context of this chapter I will confine my meaning to one of a far more intimate, close, and affectionate nature than its popular translation. In my definition most people have only a very few real friends.

Beware of making close friends in the work place. By all means establish bonds based on mutual interest and respect, with frequent contact outside the office as well as in. Avoid deeper levels of familiarity and intimacy, particularly with colleagues that you could one day find yourself in charge of. If you end up forming a friendship within my strict definition of the term, you could one day find yourself in a position of having a profound effect on their career, affecting promotion prospects or maybe having to dismiss them.

These would be traumatic experiences for both of you maybe leading to emotional conflict that could affect your judgement regarding the situation. Think ahead; avoid the possibility of burdening yourself with potential problems of this sort. Stick as far as possible to relationships based only on shared objectives and mutual respect and interests. Carefully avoid allowing them to become too close.

If this advice sounds too severe, I can only assure you it is based on considerable understanding and knowledge of the problems that can arise. I have observed too many difficulties caused by the intrusion of close friendships into a business relationship.

It may sound cold-blooded, but if you are determined to climb to the top you will at some stage or other have to act with what others might describe as a high degree of ruthlessness. If a friend happens to be on the wrong end of it, you will, if you have the normal quota of human emotions, be faced with regrets that would better have been anticipated and avoided.

SPREADING YOUR MESSAGE

As you grow in confidence, as you continue to impact favourably on the prosperity of your company or that of the division, the department or whatever unit you work in, then do not neglect to involve your colleagues in the process. Share your 'success' with them. Learn to help and develop other people's skills and abilities as you yourself progress up the ladder.

By sharing some of the credit, whilst being seen as possessing initiative coupled with obvious team spirit, you will display some of your exceptional qualities, and, very important, do so without alienating everyone around you. The greatest stars in team games are also very much the best team players.

SUPERIOR LEADERS USE SUPERIOR JUDGEMENT AVOIDING SITUATIONS REQUIRING THEIR SUPERIOR DIPLOMACY

Learn to bring out the best in those around you. Never be in a hurry to claim the credit. Inevitably it will emerge if you are benefiting your colleagues by improving their team's performance, making their work more interesting or in other ways more rewarding. Establish and maintain a common sense and a no-nonsense approach. Help your colleagues believe in the team they are part of...
... help them believe in themselves...

Use your superior listening, understanding, communication, and leadership skills to enhance your team's job satisfaction. Maintain a relentless level of intense enthusiasm. In the final result your efforts should become reflected in their increasing belief in you, and establish that vital mutual respect found where there is successful leadership.

KEY POINTS

*   Lack of individual accountability - a need to be led
*   Psychology - leadership tool - can give you an edge
*   More mouth - less fist - better communication
*   Stick to ambitions - not short term gains
*   Image your trademark - use it - don't flaunt it
*   Leadership is success - success brings rewards
*   Sight and sound - don't listen but not hear
*   Body language may deceive - look for hidden emotions
*   Unforgivable sin - betraying a confidence
*   Strictly confidential - between you and your mentor
*   Acquaintance, pal, comrade, companion - seldom friend
*   Share success - don't keep it to yourself
*   Common sense and no-nonsense approach
*   Superior judgement saves your superior skills for when they are really needed

FIVE
Self-confidence

Self-confidence is something you must possess if you are to be an effective leader. You cannot hope to be consistently successful without it. I have dwelt briefly with the subject in an earlier chapter when considering the skills, talents and personal characteristics required for leadership. Being such a keystone requirement it deserves and gets this chapter devoted exclusively to the subject.

Many resign themselves too readily to their apparent lack of self-confidence using its absence as an excuse for failure. Others claim they possess the quality whilst privately suspecting that they do not. Even so, thankfully all is not lost.

As in most things we all possess some degree of self-confidence to begin with. This can either diminish or improve with use and experience, depending quite bluntly, on how we handle ourselves in the various situations where the commodity is important.

What self-confidence we start out with is not a physical part of us such as sight or hearing, something destined to deteriorate through damage or the ageing process. It can and should, along with experience and our total fund of knowledge, improve and increase, as we grow older.

Fortunately it is predominately a mental attitude, a commodity reinforced by courage, presentation, and acting ability. In many instances the act becomes the reality and the line between a slick well-presented performance becomes so blurred that neither actor nor audience can distinguish between the role-playing and the real personality.

You can learn self-confidence, develop it and eventually project it so convincingly that one day neither you or anyone else will be able to confidently identify whether it is real or just a very convincing bluff. Eventually it all becomes self-confidence whether natural or acquired. It ceases to matter which...
... it is the result that counts...

Projection of self-confidence comprises a very wide ranging collection of signals, messages and indicators of many forms, encapsulated in a certain package or image and delivered with style. You will not gain it overnight but like so many other worthwhile skills it requires practice and application on a continuous basis. Even if you are one of the lucky ones starting out with a large slice of the spontaneous natural variety, you will still benefit from careful explorative exercise over the years, enabling you to further develop and perfect its presentation.

In this chapter I will with your co-operation, explore and develop many aspects of how you can display self-confidence to the rest of the world. In doing so I will probably be critical of some areas of your present image, presentation or life-style.

It is not the intention of this book to foster self-congratulation amongst its readers, more to encourage you to think about and to review important details of your approach and your qualifications to lead others. Nothing will be accomplished without a little pain. Now let us move on.

YOU HAVE TO HELP YOURSELF

To successfully improve your self-confidence you have to help yourself. No one else can do it all for you.

It is a little like giving up smoking or drinking. You have to want to do it, and you have to want to do it very much indeed in order to succeed. No one else can accomplish it for you. The process requires a high degree of discipline and will power.

Many of the changes you may need to make to yourself will be on a full time twenty-four hours per day basis. They are not just things you can practice and attend to during working hours. You are attempting a degree of personality change. The discipline required is part of the process that will increase your self-confidence and can be tough as indeed can any worthwhile accomplishment.

APPEARANCE

Whether we like it or not, one's physical appearance, that combination of bearing, looks, posture, clothing, cleanliness, and grooming in general, is the first impression we make when meeting strangers and inflicts an on-going impression on those we meet regularly.

Whenever we walk into a room, appear on a screen or meet someone new - our visual appearance makes a statement about ourselves - and affects how seriously new are taken - the very way which we are perceived. It is no accident that so much of the world's industrial output is devoted to products directly affecting the way we look. Even in the most impoverished and 'backward' societies, strong visual statements first and foremost communicate status and general importance.

If we were all forced to conduct our business affairs in the nude, then the study of body language would no doubt have progressed far beyond today's superficial interpretations. We would no doubt have evolved it to a far higher degree as a form of communication if we did not have as a prop.

One of my more minor ambitions is to conduct a body language training session insisting all the participants attend naked. It would prove a very interesting and enlightening exercise. The use of clothes, make-up, jewellery and other adornments steered body language into an evolutionary cul-de-sac, in my opinion stealing some of its vocabulary. I acknowledge some arguments claiming that such clothes and accessories are merely body language extensions, but I prefer and intend to consider them as separate subjects.

Again I reiterate that every time we walk into a room, appear on a screen or meet new people we make a statement about ourselves - I cannot emphasise it too strongly.

VISUAL AIDS

It is all too easy to claim that appearance should not make any difference to the way in which we view or judge others. There is a great deal of logic in that argument. The answer unfortunately is swayed by the vast amounts our population spends on improving individual visual impact. Only the naive would claim that we buy clothes just to keep ourselves warm, dry, or even 'decent'. Almost everyone, with the exception to the poorest amongst us, rarely keep clothes for their full usable life, preferring to replace them as the whims of fashion dictate.

Many of our clothes are not even designed or made to last. Manufacturers exploit our desire to continually modify and vary our appearance in order to impress, to make an impact on others. The same policy applies to many of the other accessories we collect around us.

Fashion, in particular the visual appearance of our possessions, the latest electronic notebook or portable 'phone, expensive cars, jewellery, are all important props helping us make that statement about ourselves, our status, our confidence.

Whether we like it or not, others will read these visual clues when making an early and often formative assessment of us. We cannot avoid exposure to this process. Therefore acknowledge and attend to it.

PRIDE

Are you proud of the way you look? Not everybody conforms to the 'desired' stereotypes of figure, hair and face, so avidly promoted by the media. Fortunately the 'ideal' is not absolutely necessary. Just as well, as for most of us it is not achievable. However are you confident you are respected for being fit, neat of figure, the care with which you are turned out?

How you present yourself to others?

If we have dealings with other people and we cannot be bothered to appear clean, well dressed and generally presentable, then is this not a form of insult to those we meet?

Are you really prepared to deliberately insult your customers and your colleagues in this way?

Being overweight is widely and justifiably considered unhealthy. Dirty fingernails show an obvious lack of hygiene. Scruffy stained clothes signal laziness and lack or care or lack of commitment. If someone cares so little for their own health and welfare by indicating that they could be unhealthy or dirty, then how can they be expected to take care of others?

Is that the sign of a leader? The slob you see may be the most self-confident person in the world but is certainly not projecting that impression. Self-confidence has to be presented in an attractive package if its full potential is to be exploited.

PUBLIC APPEARANCES
BODY LANGUAGE AND IMAGE

When meeting others, particularly in a business situation - do not sink into the chair. Sit up and keep back straight. You need to be comfortable…
… at the same time appearing alert…

Try to look relaxed and calm by breathing regularly. This sends the message that you are in control. Keep hand movements to the minimum. Don't fiddle with notes etc. When standing do not 'jump about'. Try to keep in one place. Think before you speak. Take your time - do not be rushed.

Respect others at all times – even if you totally disagree with them. Any loss of control or even your 'cool', gives a victory to another particularly in the battleground of a negotiation. Resist any tendency to 'talk across' others. You may see it as winning but a client will not.

KEEPING CALM BEFORE APPOINTMENTS OR MEETINGS

Check that you know exactly where you are meant to be and at what time. Aim to be early so you arrive fully in control. If you are not five minutes early then you are late. Always know the name of who you are seeing and their position in the organisation.

IN A STUDIO

In this media dominated information age you will from time to time - perhaps regularly - find yourself in a studio. It is itself a skill - requiring rather more than just care in your appearance.

Always turn off mobile phones. Once fitted with a microphone - remember everything you say can be heard. Always assume equipment is 'live'. Never relax and drop your guard. You can't always be sure where cameras may be located.

Expect surprise questions even if you have been briefed beforehand. Never ever lose your temper or even become agitated - always stay cool. Keeping calm is much more effective. Remember to say 'good morning' or 'good evening' at the start - always thank the other parties at the end.

After a successful interview it is a good idea to contact someone of influence at the studio and thank them – either by 'phone or a card. This confirms the relationship for the future and gives the opportunity to check they hold your details on file.

Being remembered for good etiquette and politeness will help others remember you, your product or service and your image.

CLOTHES - GENERAL

Be traditional - a well fitting suit preferably or a blazer or other smart jacket worn with a shirt and tie is a good choice for men and a smart skirt, blouse and jacket for ladies - who should also avoid showing too much flesh either above or below the waist.

Men should choose medium to dark colours – but not black – nothing that that looks at all like a uniform. Avoid strong stripes or patterns. A classic English pinstripe is always acceptable.

Coloured shirts give a warmer more approachable image. White is not good – especially on TV. Ties can be patterned, plain or striped. Choose warm colours. Avoid jumpers or cardigans – much too casual. They give the impression that you do not care- that what you are doing is not important.

Tweeds, jeans and cords are the same – too relaxed, out doors and scruffy. Avoid – unless being interviewed on a farm in the mud.

Most of the above applies to both men and women.

Ladies also need to take care in the choice of jewellery, scarves and frills – keep it simple. Beware of sparkly, shiny and shimmering fabrics during daytime. Large patterns or black and white are too bold, especially in photographs or on TV.

Tailored shapes always look more positive and business-like. Trousers can be worn if you are sure the occasion is right. A medium length skirt is always safe.

Shoes should be understated, not too high and boots must be chosen with care. They are often not ideal indoors.

It is important to control hair. If hair is long, have a plan for windy days - hair band, plait or ponytail - or even a hat. Try them out before you need them...
... be prepared...

Make up needs to be subtle and well applied - not too bright. Warm muted shades work best. Only apply what you are happy with. You must feel comfortable and be yourself - but give a groomed and confident air.

Try outfits beforehand. Experiment with make up and hair - so you are ready when it's needed.

I make no apology for again mentioning the importance of you initial visual impact the statement you make every time you walk into a room - appear on a screen - or meet someone new. First impressions remain vital and establish an immediate image affecting the perceptions others form of you.

SO EASY

Factors such as weight and overall fitness are comparatively easy to put right. Firstly consider hygiene and grooming. Never let anyone have an excuse for thinking that you fall short of the highest standards in this department. Many people do not realise it when they have a hygiene problem. This applies especially in senior jobs or 'high pressure' ones, where stress and other excitement can trigger off unforeseen and unfortunate glandular excretions.

Leave nothing to chance in this area. Personally I have for many years enjoyed bathing at least twice a day. I use the event as an opportunity for reflection as well as relaxation. My morning bath provides me with a superb chance to ponder the likely events of the working day ahead. In doing so I can quietly consider my possible reactions to them. My evening bath, whilst important for unwinding, also gives me time to review the day's happenings and re-appraise them.

At times of intense activity, such as when I first extended my company's market to the USA, I would often, despite the pressures on my time, take a break during the middle of the day and retire to my hotel for a quick shower. Again giving me a chance for recapitulation and reflection it would cleanse, refresh and cool me in preparation for another few hours in the steam bath atmosphere of a New York August. It was a worthwhile investment in both time and effort. Followed by a change of underwear and shirt I would then re-enter the fray, cooler more comfortable and relaxed, a definitely more self-confident salesman.

SPARES

Wherever I may be I always have a spare shirt and necktie either in my briefcase or 'filed' in the office. You can never tell when some accident with a coffee cup or a prawn sandwich will render one of them essential. Women should always of course carry spare tights or stockings in their handbags as well as a 'top up' for their make-up.

Always plan and prepare what you intend to wear at least one day ahead. When considering whom I am scheduled or likely to meet and the impression I wish to create, I always put much thought into the suit I intend to wear. Understanding that my choice of clothes can influence my mood for the day, it is a worthwhile exercise.

Because the garments invariably need attention such as brushing and pressing, they should be selected sufficiently far ahead for the necessary valeting and not in haste on the morning required. Obviously when travelling on business your planning and choice becomes particularly important due to the restrictions of your luggage capacity.

IF YOU LOOK GOOD - YOU WILL FEEL GOOD

My intention is not to advise on the specific choice of clothes for others - I am not the most qualified to do so and am happy to leave it to experts such as my wife who is an authority on that subject.

I am aware of the items I look good in, the ones I prefer to wear, and the things that give my self-confidence a definite upward flip. You should put considerable thought into the subject yourself however I will suggest a few guidelines.

Obviously avoid extremes of fashion. They are always controversial. Buy the best quality you can afford but consistent with your need to possess a good selection to cater for differing occasions. Make sure you understand and practice good coordination of both colour and style. Failure to achieve this will convey the impression of being disjointed and badly organised in other areas, possibly including your work.

Develop a thorough comprehensive wardrobe in keeping with the places you visit and the functions you attend. Quality is more important than quantity as long as you have enough items to give variety to your appearance.

Make sure everything you wear starts off clean and well pressed with all the buttons present. If you anticipate a situation that might affect your general elegance such as a long aircraft journey, select clothes that are less likely to become creased and crumpled.

There is nothing worse than arriving three-hundred miles from your base for an important meeting feeling hot, sweaty - with creases in your suit, a grubby damp shirt, and not being able to do much about it.

Select a suit that does not crease too readily. Wash your face and change into a clean shirt at the destination airport if you do not have access to a hotel room or similar facility. Obviously make allowances in your schedule for such personal needs. Although it might seem impressive to be so busy you cannot find time to do these things, you would be foolish not to make space for them. It is certainly not time wasted, as you will function more effectively if you feel fresh, clean, and self-confident.

Similarly it is essential to allow time to shower and change your clothes before an evening engagement. It gives one's confidence a terrific psychological boost if attending a perhaps confrontational, after hours meeting, knowing that you are refreshed and dressed in a completely fresh set of clothes.

It feels particularly good if you are meeting with others who quite obviously are showing signs of having sat in the same things all day.

If facilities for taking a shower shortly before an evening meeting are unavailable to you, make sure you have at least washed your face and have changed all your clothes or at minimum your shirt, before attending. I assume that everyone these days keeps a shoe cleaning kit in their office and of course uses it. It is not so easy to get a shoeshine in the UK as it is in New York. I always spent a fortune there...
... grabbing a quick shoeshine between meetings...

Not only will you feel much better, much more prepared, but also you then know that you have at least been thorough in your physical preparation. You have done all you can in that area and can then concentrate on mental preparation.

Your appearance will also signal to colleagues who had seen you looking different earlier in the day, your degree of seriousness and indicate your level of preparation and organisation. They will naturally think that at least an equal level of detail has gone into the mental side of your make up.

HAIR AND HANDS

Hands are one of the most important tools we use in non-verbal communication. Try describing any complex situation whilst keeping your hands in your pockets and you will understand exactly what I mean. To do so effectively and consistently would require much practice.

Hands are highly visible and much noticed. I previously commented that dirty fingernails or indeed grubby hands, whether resulting from nicotine or just plain dirt, are an absolute no go area. Remember others do not just see our hands. They touch them, handshakes on meeting and on parting. It is an insult if to were expected to touch a filthy paw.

Another unforgivable flaw and an especially unattractive one, is the possession of bitten fingernails. The visual evidence of this habit disgusts many people. Widely considered an indication of nervousness and insecurity it certainly signals an appalling lack of self-control. It is hardly an advertisement for cool, calm self-confidence.

TOPPING IT ALL

Regardless of whether you are male or female you must devote time and attention to your hair. The style and condition yet again gives very strong signals about you as a person. Women of course have a very considerable advantage in this department, as they do in most other areas of personal appearance. For them the variety of style and availability of expert advice is far greater.

Avoid your hairstyle sending the wrong message. Even the simple difference of a woman wearing her long hair up during the working day, then reappearing with it down at an evening function, can convey a distinct and possibly wrong message. Think about it. Do you want to 'let your hair down' in the evening when work is involved, or should you maintain a 'business image'…
… the decision is yours…

Hairstyle can also be used to reinforce an image. Many well-known politicians, businessmen, and 'celebrities' have hung onto out-dated styles that help to establish an image or trademark, readily and easily grasped by the media. Businessmen with loud kipper ties, politicians with blond flowing locks, and film stars with completely clean-shaven heads all subscribe to this philosophy.

A well-cut and carefully styled head of hair says a great deal about the person underneath. It indicates that you care about yourself and wish to make a good impression on others. Never choose a style that is difficult to control. Make sure it is always clean and does not look greasy. On no account show evidence of dandruff or dry scalp. If necessary wash your hair every morning if that is what it takes to avoid such pitfalls.

If your hair colour is not natural, on no account neglect its maintenance allowing the natural colour to be detected. There is nothing that looks quite so tatty as blond hair with dark roots. Work with your hairdresser to find a cut that can be maintained with the minimum effort in line with your schedules.

FACES

We always notice eyes first. Bright clear eyes certainly give the impression of a bright clear mind. We cannot always control this factor but we can certainly influence it by having enough sleep and by moderating our alcohol consumption the night before. Alcohol and stress are both factors most affecting eye clarity. One of these at least is under your control.

If you wear spectacles there are a large variety of designs to choose from. You have no excuse for not selecting a pair that will enhance the image you choose to convey. Remember also the value of removing your glasses at certain times in a meeting or presentation. Use them to punctuate some of the points you are making. They can be used as a very effective prop.

Teeth are the second most important facial consideration. Discoloured teeth are in a similar league to dirty fingernails. There is absolutely no excuse for them. Apart from the negative visual image they convey, bad teeth often are connected with halitosis, something that would definitely affect your image in a negative way. It will definitely not make you popular with colleagues and will give them ammunition for some very disrespectful jokes. The wide availability of dental treatment makes problems in this area inexcusable.

Make-up is a very personal and important decision for a female and well beyond the scope of this book and its author. You and you alone can decide how much if any, make-up you wish to use. Obviously be particularly aware of the use and possibilities provided by make-up. Learn the basic techniques so if you feel it can at times enhance your image, and then you are confident and competent in using it…
… if necessary take professional advice…

Facial hair is a subject I take very personally. I have a full beard. Such facial hair is still widely considered undesirable. It is still perceived by many as an attempt to hide behind something, a mask perhaps. By others is considered just plain dirty.

The body language pundits claim beards create an opportunity for displaying visual signs of nervousness. The theory is that a nervous bearded person will display his emotions by fiddling with his facial hair. Therefore if you do not have one you will almost certainly show it in some other way. I personally believe anti-beard discrimination to be despicable. As I said, I am prejudiced as someone who sports a beard.

Personally I feel more self-confidence with my beard. It gives my face a better shape, and makes me look younger. Many members of the opposite sex have told me I am better looking with a beard. Vanity aside I really feel better with it and therefore I go against conventional wisdom and retain my beard.

I always keep it neatly trimmed and tidy, and make sure I wash it at least twice per day. Obviously it is a very personal decision, but if in doubt and you are intent on projecting the most widely acceptable image - then stay clean-shaven.

JEWELLERY

Jewellery sends strong visual signals extending and exaggerating the image you are trying to portray. Rightly or wrongly we have come to associate certain items and combinations with popular stereotypes. For example a chunky gold identity chain and gold sovereign rings would be expected on a man who is a used car dealer or boxing promoter, whilst a Cartier three band ring signals a woman who has confident good taste to others who share similar interests.

The huge chunky traditional gold Rolex watch with its bracelet pattern identifiable at a range of half a mile is now so associated with flashy 'look I've made it' attitudes, and so imitated with cheap but detailed copies, that it has lost ground to equally expensive but more subtle designs from other manufacturers.

Much of the clothes and accessories available for both sexes are so specialised in their message, that they communicate their true affluence and taste only too a small and privileged sector. Jewellery is a badge stating what group we believe we belong to.

The used car dealer's heavy gold bracelet and chunky gold Rolex display his success but say nothing about his taste and judgement. They are now so readily identifiable that all they say is 'expensive'.

The highly self-confident individual, intent on or already in the top job, will want to show he or she knows what is tasteful, high quality, and sometimes what is in vogue. Their statement will be one of discrete and considered impact, not one of ostentation.

SEEK ADVICE

Many aspects of personal presentation are specialist subjects and beyond the scope of this publication. I urge you to take expert advice. There are literally hundreds of books and magazines covering these subjects. It is surprising why so many of us fail to make the most of our appearance. The answer has to be that a large section of the population just do not care enough - however if you wish to project the maximum image of self-confidence then you will have to care whether you like it or not. It is part of the job.

Make the most of the people you already know and deal with. You have experts in your dentist, your doctor, hairdresser etc. Ask questions and involve them. You will be amazed how willing they will be to help. Nothing is gained by leaving things to chance. No one you ever see looking great and self-confident has got there purely by chance. It will have taken them an enormous amount of time, effort, thought and practice.

If you feel, after having made a list of all the areas of your personal appearance needing attention, that your task is too formidable a one, then on no account try to rectify everything at one go. Re-arrange your list in order of the priority you attach to each of these items and the sequence in which you intend tackling them. Take them one or two at a time, gaining experience and confidence as you do so...

... you will be surprised how much progress you will make...

DOES YOUR APPEARANCE COMPLIMENT OR INSULT

Do not be afraid to show others around you that you are spending time and money attending to your appearance. It will demonstrate to them that you care enough about their opinions to go to substantial trouble to look good and to feel good. It is a compliment to others if you go to a lot of trouble to look your best in their presence. Not to do so is insulting. Knowing that you are scoring highly in this department gives you a general feeling of well being with an obvious benefit to your self-confidence.

If you do not respect yourself, how on earth can you expect anyone else to respect you or even take you seriously?

THE RIGHT MENTAL ATTITUDE

On the preceding pages I concentrated on the more visual presentation factors affecting self-confidence together with how others perceive it and how we view ourselves. These, however important, are just the packaging around the product. We should now address what is inside the package.

Some very rare and lucky people are born believing they can do virtually anything. Others benefit from expensive education not primarily to develop their academic skills, more to brainwash them into assuming they belong to a class possessing the right to govern, control, and in effect run the lives of others.

Such training, however expensive, is fundamentally flawed. It forms only part of the equation. That equation simply stated, shows that for every leader there must be someone to lead, or more usually, several others prepared to be led

Unfortunately these very expensively educated, traditionally prepared and packaged leaders are a product of a system evolved when we needed to administer a huge empire. Although having predominately run our establishment, our institutions and our largest companies, they are now increasingly facing a credibility problem.

We live after all, in the 'information age'. Folk in general are not as easily fooled as they once were. More and more we can see through the gloss and look for the substance underneath.

Most people are no longer so ready to respond to the trappings of authority, listen to the educated voice, or defer to someone because of who their father is! They want leadership in line with the characteristics described in Chapter One. No longer acceptable is the 'divine right' of certain social classes to run things, to hog the best jobs and the positions of influence. We are learning to look for and to relate to...
... the true person inside the package...

If our packaging is not good we have a severe handicap. The package has to be attended to, make no mistake. It is relatively easy to get right and important enough not to be neglected. The mental attitude underneath the packaging, particularly if you start from a position of low self-confidence, is the more difficult area to tackle.

EVERYONE HAS ACHIEVEMENTS

Achievement is a 'relative' commodity. If we all measured our personal achievements against some absolute universal yardstick, then no one would ever be satisfied they had achieved anything. I call this the 'ambition of the receding horizon'. Consider if your sights were focused metaphorically, on reaching some imaginary horizon. You never get there. As you approach your original observed objective the horizon, effectively always receding, exposes another target further away. You re-tune your ambition…
… you never become satisfied…

When I was much younger my receding horizon concept was part of my motivation. I never expected to be completely happy or totally satisfied with my progress. As soon as I came close to achieving my current objectives I would move the receding horizon of my ambitions further away from me - more difficult to reach. It seemed a very good idea at the time and certainly ensured that I worked long and hard. Probably it made me in some ways a very boring person, an obsessed single-minded workaholic.

Gradually it dawned on me that there were other things in life besides money and work. Balanced involvement in other activities would not just make my life much more interesting, but by giving me a broader outlook and encouraging me to be less obsessive about my work, would improve the aspects of my character and personality important in leading others.

SMELL THE ROSES ALONG THE WAY

So do not set your ambitions so high that they are in reality unattainable. Make sure there are enough perhaps lesser ones along the way for some successes always to be within reach. You must have achievements and triumphs along the way. Make sure you take a little time to savour the experience. Do not be so quick to re-set your ambitions so that like my receding horizon, you never stay close enough to an achievement to pause for a moment and enjoy the experience. Too much dedication at the exclusion of everything else can leave a curiously empty feeling. Success is meaningless unless it is enjoyed…

… leave time enough to smell the roses along the way...

I confess to be lucky enough always to have had what many others have described as an 'over abundance of self-confidence'. It does not of course apply to every department of my life. I am for example a poor swimmer and would be a lousy tennis player, and I remain totally incompetent at DIY. Accepting such inadequacies I avoid having to rely on them.

Consequently recognising my shortcomings if I am in a situation where I might be forced to swim, perhaps in a life or death survival situation, which could arise in the event of engine failure whilst flying a single engined aircraft over water, then I take care always to wear a life jacket and to have a survival dinghy within reach. I never play tennis, squash, football, or do any of the others things I am not good at. Not surprisingly I find I enjoy doing the things I am good at far more than the other sort. There is little point in wasting time on activities that I do not do well and do not particularly enjoy.

Most of us obtain much more satisfaction and reward applying such policies to our leisure time. It is a tragedy of universal proportions that so many of the world's population spend their lives in jobs where they experience little satisfaction and happiness.

VIRTUOUS CIRCLE

Apart from the negative contribution this miss-fit of ability and skills have caused and continues to cause in stimulating industrial disputes, malcontent, bad service and poor productivity, it is just such a tragic waste of human resources and time.

We all tend be much better at the activities we enjoy, and obviously enjoy the things we are good at. There must be some better system at matching aptitude to job and by doing so making so many lives so much more fulfilling. In turn the spin-off from improved service and efficiency would be incalculable.

A virtuous circle rather than a vicious one…

My final school report conclude with the words: "Hunter has spent the last five years doing precisely what he wanted to do and not what the school wished him to do. He must realise that he cannot go through the rest of his life following such a philosophy".

It was the final little dig from a headmaster unable to bring himself to say anything good about one of his star troublemakers, as I was about to be launched at the tender age of sixteen into my 'career' as the village postman. It annoyed me intensely. Resolving to prove his prediction wrong, I have so far successfully carried out the philosophy he considered so undesirable.

Life has a very short span. Surely we must be more selective in what we do. Concentrate as much as possible on the things we do well. In doing so we are likely to be more successful in materiel terms and far more contented on a personal level.

No doubt due to my selectivity in what I have done with my life both in the work arena and in my leisure activities, I have never bothered to spend much time in working on my own self-confidence. Particularly in business matters I have always adopted the attitude that if someone else could do something then so could I. It sounds arrogant but that is the way it was.

Any misgivings I might have had in the self-confidence department were invariably swept aside in the slipstream arising from the blast of enthusiasm I whipped up over new endeavours.

This admission does not in any way dilute or diminish my qualifications to write this chapter. Having spent a very considerable proportion or my working life building up the self-confidence in others, and in doing it very much in keeping with my title theme, that of leading others by showing them and helping them believe more in themselves. It is also a process that once you begin to communicate to others, they then learn, adapt, and themselves pass on.

A reaction is triggered whereby they start to evolve and believe in their own leadership skills. It is an extremely simple, common sense, no nonsense approach, and a quite obvious adoption of a mental attitude. I consider it a fundamental discipline and training in building the most effective teams possible.

STARTING THE PROCESS

To start the process of building up your own mental self-confidence you must first make a list of your most significant achievements in your life to date.

Your skills and your qualities, the things you have accomplished that you are most proud of. Many folk due to embarrassment, modesty, or perhaps other reasons, have trouble getting such a list started. Such reluctance in getting the list going is not helped by my insistence on at least fifty items, two pages of A4 with twenty-five per page…
… try it…

If you find it difficult to think of at least fifty items, then you are probably excluding some because you may not think they are worthy of listing. That is precisely why I am asking for the apparently high figure of fifty. It forces most people to do much 'soul searching' as well as racking their memory.

Obviously many of us have achievements that come easily to the memory. My own list would include such items as being one of the first British businessmen to set up a computer consultancy business in the USA, and one of an even smaller group who has had their operation there survive successfully for over two decades. I am fortunate in having a list of business start-ups, innovation, company turn-arounds, and other career milestones of which I remain proud.

Outside of the workplace I also am lucky enough to have done many things which have given me both a great deal of pleasure and a sense of achievement, and which I would happily repeat if the opportunity arises.

I have been fortunate to possess or evolve the self-confidence I required to do these things, but they did not occur purely by chance. I had an extremely poor start in life, and learned at a very early age the importance of the survival instinct. I am also not a particularly likeable person, and therefore I had to work hard at many of my leadership techniques.

Probably many of you will not have founded a business in the USA or indeed elsewhere, or have a similar accomplishment to feature high on your list. You may not even have anything that you feel would be worth mentioning in company of others you regard as successful. In interviewing applicants for director level or senior manager positions I have been amazed at the inability of many candidates in listing any worthwhile accomplishments at all.

DON'T WRITE YOURSELF OFF TOO SOON

I remain convinced that we are so indoctrinated by the media in hearing about self-made millionaires, multimillionaire pop stars, and heads of multinational corporations, that the concept of solid, rewarding but unspectacular success is being overlooked by many. Indeed even classified as non-events. We are continually urged to aim so high to aspire to so much, that many of us are prematurely writing ourselves off as failures, or being written off by others.

I recall one of the sayings we had at the tail end of the nineteen sixties. It was: "If you haven't made it by the time you are thirty, you never will". The trouble is many believed it, lost motivation, and the world was denied of much of their talent. More importantly others believed it and prematurely wrote off excellent people who did not appear to have measured up to some arbitrary achievement level within some equally arbitrary timescale.

It is a trap that many are still falling into. Far too much of our experience and talent is discarded through not conforming to measurements and requirements that in the end have little to do with the objectives being pursued. Mediocrity breeds mediocrity. It is a destructive parasite of a plant and once it has taken hold in an organisation it becomes very difficult for competence to become dominant again.

Again we come back to my insistence on a two-page list consisting of at least fifty items. I insist on this list even if item forty-nine is 'coming third in the village egg and spoon race at the age of seven'. I did precisely this and it still pleases me. Why? My objective was to beat my rival Roger. He came forth...
… therefore I was a success…

Write your list. We all have to begin the process somewhere.

When you have listed your fifty items you are now in a position to start to review it. Take your time. Spread the process over two or three days. You will find yourself adding to the list, dropping some items off the bottom as you recall other more worthy ones.

Continually rearrange the sequence of the items. Put them in order of what you regard as the most worthwhile, laudable, or important to what you want to become.

CAST YOUR NET WIDE

Are you artistic? Good at sport? Humorous? Or can you dance, act or sing? Are you a natural storyteller? Do you have a way with the written word? Can you do complicated mental arithmetic, or do you have a flair for algebra? Do you play a musical instrument; have you performed as a member of a pop group however amateur? Are you an engaging public speaker, or active at some political level? Were you very successful at school?

Have you ever started or run any sort of business venture however modest in your spare time, even if it was selling buns at a profit to the others at school? Is there anything you have invented? Have you organised any events requiring the leadership of others?

It all counts somewhere. Everybody can compile fifty items if they try hard enough...
... start somewhere...

Review all aspects and stages of your life to date in making this list. You should make it up to fifty items however ordinary they may seem to you. Remember it is a very private review you are undertaking. Show it to no one. There should be no one else present to judge it, to look down at what you have done, to measure it against his or her own achievements or to ridicule you in any way.

Your list is a private, introspective catalogue, your starting point, however impressive or otherwise. It is what you have achieved so far, not what you intend to do or where you are going. A starting point only.

Your continual reappraisal and re-ordering of the relative importance of the listed items will over a period of a few days, bring some surprises. Not only will you constantly change the order of the first page, the most important twenty-five items, but also you will be amazed how many new items you will remember in time.

It is quite astonishing how different the final list that emerges is from the first one. Very few of us keep our best, certainly not our fifty most important achievement, triumphs, areas of excellence, and other personal satisfactions at the front of our minds for most of the time. Yet how can you expect to build up your self-confidence if you do not know the things you are good at, or have forgotten what you have achieved in the past?

Your initial reaction to my required list of fifty items may be one of scepticism, but try it. I will almost guarantee you will learn some worthwhile things about yourself. If evaluated intelligently they will help you start the process of improving your self-confidence.

REGULARLY UPDATE THE LIST

Many of us have a mental list, roughly corresponding to the written one I recommend. There are times when that list is consulted to prepare for a specific event or challenge that is imminent - an interview for example, or perhaps an important presentation or a public speech. If I have a speaking engagement, I mentally review my experiences of similar assignments previously undertaken, drawing comfort from my successful execution of them.

Whenever scheduled for a particularly crucial meeting with my majority shareholder, I would mentally recall my air racing days. Flying down low sometimes through appalling weather, so low I would never admit it to the Civil Aviation Authority. Pushed further than is comfortable to remember by surges of adrenalin I remember an obsession to win at almost any cost - 'blown up' engines - bird strikes - swerving to avoid a church steeple, or a cross-channel ferry. After this, business confrontations could hold little fear. Having risked my life on so many occasions racing aircraft, what did I possibly have to fear from a stressful confrontational meeting? A mere job paled into insignificance.

Whatever you put on your list, however you measure it against the accomplishments of others, remember it is private to you. Continually revise and update the list, in particular the top twenty-five items.

You will be surprised how often they change, especially in the early stages as you re-evaluate the relative importance of each and every item, and as you recall others you judge worth adding. In time as new high points and achievement occur they in turn will find their place on your list.

We all have worthwhile talents, skills, career and personal milestones of note, even if we prefer to keep many of them to ourselves. They all count. You have to start somewhere in identifying what are yours if you wish to improve your self-confidence...
... begin the process now...

FAILURE

I have not given much space to this subject. There is very little point in devoting too much mental capacity to cataloguing one's failures. We all have some. It is no use denying them. We must obviously try to turn each one into the maximum positive benefit.

Learn from each failure and why it occurred. Learn from them about any lapse of concentration, attention to detail, descents into complacency etc, which contributed to the failures occurring. Above all do not let a failure dilute your self-confidence. Learn then move on turning each lesson into some future success.

Some failures will be of such a magnitude that their disclosure to others can severely damage the image of a very self-confident leader. The rather sensitive issue of personal relationships particularly marriage, is the most relevant here. A strong lobby exists to play down the significance of a disastrous divorce or other marital failure.

Not surprisingly the main motivation behind this lobby stems form those most likely to be damaged by the truth, the alarmingly numerous percentage of the population that directly experience marital breakdown. Logical examination of the problem would suggest that its significance should in no way be under estimated.

VALUE OF A GOOD MARRIAGE

Consider the list of achievements I have advocated you make. I suggest that a really good marriage should deserve to rank very highly near the top of everybody's list. It is for most of us the major event in our lives. Its success or failure affects our emotional and often our physical health, and can determine the level of energy, ambition and determination that we apply to our working lives.

It has to be said that the aftermath of a divorce for example, can have a very positive rather than a negative effect, releasing energy into one's work, and inspiring ambitions that remained dormant whilst the marital problems were being sorted out. I have known numerous situations where the aftermath of a difficult and acrimonious divorce resulted in an avalanche of ambition, determination and productivity from individuals previously lukewarm in their approach to their careers. Some people feel after a marital breakdown that they have to prove something, and their work subsequently benefits.

The fact remains that an unhappy marriage is usually the result of a seriously bad decision, a failure in our major 'career' our life. What is more it is a failure of disastrous significance for all but the most cynical and insensitive - one that will not go away or be forgotten easily. The logic is obvious. Marriage is a very serious step to make...
... probably the major one in most lives...

If you select the wrong partner, and I do not under estimate the problems in finding the right one, then you have initiated a problem that sooner or later will have to be rectified in a process that is usually time consuming, financially very expensive, emotionally draining and often eroding to one's dignity.

Too many marry very early, usually for the wrong, often predominantly sexual reasons. The most totally and ruthlessly ambitious would wait until they found a partner they were sure they would be proud of when they reached the top job - someone who would be a career asset.

Far too many 'out-grow' partners in both work and social achievement after originally imagining they would remain happy with them forever. Many others never really give the long-term implications much consideration. Their partners are then discarded or deserted in favour of a new one more in keeping with their current needs and status.

If your marriage fails or your partner does not meet your current 'standards', there will be an ongoing cost in permanent emotional scarring and damage to your mental health. In addition you will be demonstrating to all who are witness to the situation that your judgement is highly suspect on important matters. You will also have a major failure on your record.

I recognise that in stating these opinions I am likely to upset at least fifty percent of my readers, but facts are facts. When we come down to the basic logic, if you cannot get something right that is such a fundamental, major, and important part of your life, then how can your be expected to possess and exercise superior judgement on business matters?

You may argue that business considerations are not as important as personal relationships or that the decisions are not so difficult. That may or may not be true. The shareholders, taxpayers, or whoever your ultimate employers are, may take a different viewpoint. Why should they believe they could trust you to look after their commercial interests if you cannot even run your own life successfully?

LEARN FROM FAILURES

Learn from failures. Not just why or how they occur but the effect they have on others. Make sure the people you lead see clearly what you are learning and how you intend to turn those lessons into positive assets in the future.

Whilst on such subjects it is important to avoid any other aspects of your personal life that could elicit disapproval, from becoming public. Remember that most people have double standards of morality. Whatever they personally do or would like to do is not necessarily acceptable to those they lead or those who lead them.

Observation of those in public life in the UK will show frequent examples of this. Every few months some new scandal erupts causing embarrassment to perhaps a notable erstwhile pillar of society, perhaps resulting in media ridicule and sometimes enforced resignation from some influential position or other.

Usually the 'crime' is not in reality the trivial mistake or sexual misdemeanour, which has been exposed, but the crime of being found out. We expect out leaders to be much 'holier' than we are.

Unfortunately there is probably more villainy committed amongst the upper echelons of major companies than ever on the streets. It is not so evident because the criminals are so much cleverer and often very powerful, whilst surrounded by well-paid sycophants with a vested interest in keeping quiet.

When the scandals erupt they become massive and fascinating, gathering the same mass hysterical audience that might once have attended public executions. The same people who stand silently by, observing their leader's abuse of power and authority will be the first to bay for blood when a fall is imminent. It seldom occurs to them that by their own indifference or fear of dissenting they are at least involved in the corruption.

Be aware how merciless the world will be if when reaching the top you are eventually exposed as lacking in the morals department. The old adage "the bigger they are the harder they fall" is often only too true.

If you indulge in activities that might not meet with general approval then keep them to yourself. Although boasting about them to your mates and acquaintances might make you feel good for a while, you will regret it eventually as events inevitably and embarrassingly leak out to a wider, less than appreciative world.

Watch your drinking habits. Even if you do not have a alcohol problem, but more importantly if you do, then exercise extreme moderation in the company of colleagues and other business contacts. Ignore how much others drink. Stay sober. Listen to and take in what the others say. Exploit the willingness shown by many to part with useful information when their tongues are 'loosened' by drink. You will obtain much helpful knowledge on their true feelings and about the prevailing opinions around them.

Your best position is not to drink at all where there are work contacts present. If you feel you need to have to drink to be sociable, keep it down to one or two glasses only.

Never drink hoping or believing it will temporarily reinforce your level of self-confidence. Alcohol, although maybe giving you a false very short-term boost, actually has the reverse effect of diminishing your self-confidence when sober.

LIFE-STYLE

Try wherever possible to use aspects of your lifestyle to boost your self-confidence as well as your image. During a period of my life when I was lucky enough to win some minor sporting trophies, I did not hesitate to display them in my office. When after a year, some of them had to be returned to the organisers of the events, I would photograph them and display the prints. I also display other reminders of my life outside work that please me and are visually attractive. If for example you paint well, there is nothing wrong with one or two or your best works hanging on your office wall.

Trophies, photographs, and other objects that continually remind you of your achievements outside work, act as an ice breaking talking point for visitors.

In my own case they were acknowledged by my youthful team, many of who had been involved with my leisure pursuits such as air racing.

If you are good at some sporting activity do not hide it - publicise your involvement, obtain company sponsorship if possible. As long as you are not arrogant about your successes, your team at work, will take an interest in what you do and maybe derive pleasure from it. You will find they prefer to be led by a 'winner'.

If you are in any way mildly eccentric, then do not hide it unless it has some negative overtones. 'Characters' are talked about. We do not expect or indeed want our bosses to be boring non-events. If your eccentricity is harmless do not hide it...
... instead use it...

CHARISMA

It has become fashionable to use the words 'charisma' or 'charismatic' in describing many of the leaders, the 'celebrities', entertainers and many others, whose work life-style, politics or other deeds are deemed by the media to be of interest to the rest of us.

The word 'charisma' has therefore become a very commonplace perhaps over used component in our every day vocabulary. Sometimes I wonder if many of its users know what its dictionary definition is - much of the time the word is used as part of an expression with negative connotations, such as describing the boss as having 'all the charisma of a dead rat'.

When used in a positive sense 'charisma' has become a fashionable word to describe a multitude of attractive and likeable characteristics, without too much attention being focused on its literal sense. Unfortunately whatever popular definition is being used it would feature highly on most lists of desired leadership qualities, despite being more acclaimed than actually possessed. It is inevitably assumed to signal self-confidence amongst the virtues ascribed to it.

Rarely is someone described as charismatic without also being, or at least implied to be, self-confident. I cannot recall anyone being considered as lacking in self-confidence but thought to have charisma. It appears acceptable to have self-confidence without having charisma, but not charisma without self-confidence.

So desirable and highly rated is this commodity we term charisma, that it is obviously very desirable to possess it or if possible acquire it. You should therefore strive to add it to your repertoire, making it contribute towards your self-confident image...
...what do we mean by 'charisma'?

My dictionary defines it as follows:
'Capacity to inspire followers with devotion and enthusiasm'

This definition is as good as any I can find. Examination of the above definition is encouraging. Instead of an almost mystical god-given gift, it makes the commodity seem quite attainable by training and practice, even by we mere mortals.

Consider the 'inspiring others with enthusiasm' part of the definition. What is involved in achieving that? Nothing less than many of the points we have already covered under the subject of self-confidence, but mixed and delivered with tremendous enthusiasm.

It has been proved time and time again that enthusiasm is a very infectious commodity. If you apply a relentless and ongoing enthusiasm to your work and to your leadership, then it will inspire others and be taken up by them. This essential ingredient to your charisma mix is in fact one of the easiest to acquire.

The 'devotion' element is somewhat more difficult to cultivate. Devotion suggests almost a relinquishing of some control in the direction of the subject described as charismatic. It suggests perhaps an illogical trust. It hints at a relationship bordering on the emotional.

Although such intensity might occur in the case of some very high profile leaders, I suspect that it is more than usually intended when the word charismatic is written or spoken.

I propose to substitute 'deep loyalty' for devotion, as I believe it more accurately reflects the 'charisma' we are aiming to develop. We have discussed loyalty earlier in this publication. Suffice to reiterate if you practice most of the essentials of good leadership, taking care to give your team your total loyalty, they will reciprocate it. Loyalty at its most intense is a two-way bond.

In developing loyalty and inspiring enthusiasm you are well on the way to acquiring qualities to which the tag 'charisma' may well be added. The self-confident high profile leader tends to accumulate ail the qualities that others will consider charismatic. It is not some God-given gift but a commodity that you can develop and grow in line with your evolving success as a leader. There are myriad instances of this.

SELLING THE PACKAGE

Having developed and practised your self-confidence, and packaged the results into the image you wish to portray to the outside world, you have to 'sell' yourself to others at all times. On the way to the top, unless you have spare funds at your disposal, you will normally have to undertake the projection of your chosen image yourself, devoting both time and funds to it.

Once you reach the top you may be able to utilise some of your organisation's funds towards public relations or similar activities, which will project and enhance your image as well as that of the company.

Whatever stages you are at remember to maintain some basic rules. Always retain your self-respect. If you do not you will lose the respect of others. Make sure you stand out from the crowd otherwise your talents might not be so readily noticed. You may not succeed in being exciting but at least you must try to be interesting.

KEY POINTS

*   Self-confidence - keystone to success
*   The one thing that grows better with age
*   Packaging - how others see you
*   No one else can do it for you - self-confidence is a very personal affair
*   Like it or not first impressions count
*   Naked leadership - could you lead your team undressed?
*   Your appearance - does it insult those you meet?
*   Use the Boost your morale - look good, feel good
*   Experts - doctor, dentist, hairdresser, tailor
*   True leadership - not tie recognition
*   Helping others believe in themselves - positively dispels depression, disputes discontent
*   Media hype creates unrealistic ambitions
*   The right partner - the most important business decision you will ever make
*   Scandal is bad news - never forgotten - take care on the way up
*   Charisma - self-belief - belief in the team - deep loyalty and devotion - it's all very contagious
*   Whenever you walk into a room you make a statement about yourself

SIX
Leader Of The Team

Commonly teams range in and size from a few people working on a project - or staffing a small department or company - to a multinational conglomerate with one hundred thousand employees.

My dictionary defines 'team' as "a set of persons working together".

That definition suits me fine. Many management psychologists have invented much more elaborate more complex definitions, and would indeed dispute the above dictionary definition. I was not a management psychologist just an 'old country boy' trying to make a living in the big city. However for most of my working life I have been in charge of a team of some size or other.

Nobody bothered to tell me that in the opinion of some management expert or other, my teams may not have been teams at all but merely groups of people, despite all working together towards a common objective. I am very glad I did not at the time know such sophisticated definitions. They might have distracted me from my mission of turning my teams into more effective ones. They might have got in the way. My beliefs on leadership apply equally to teams of all sizes from the smallest to the very largest.

At least one well-known management psychologist puts a size limit on what he calls a team, suggesting 'small groups of typically seven or eight people'.

I cannot agree with this. As long as all members have a common purpose and are ultimately following the same leader, there is no limit to the size of the team.

There is also no reason why a very large team should not be sub-divided into many smaller teams. In fact this is one of the things traditional hierarchical structures depend upon. The concept of a team is in no way diluted by it being composed of many smaller teams.

The leaders of the smaller teams are key members reporting to the leader of a larger team. What is vital is that the objectivity is maintained irrespective of the structural size. It is fine for a small team, part of a larger organisation, having its own localised objectives; in fact it is vital that it does so. It must however keep and maintain sight of the overall objectives of the larger organisation of which it forms part.

A large company or other organisation must be one large team consisting of teams within teams to be effective.

TEAMS

The meaning of the word as I interpret it is as follows:

Team: *group of people working together with common purpose, and under one leadership.*

A team may itself be composed of a number of component teams.

This modularity is obviously essential in organisations of considerable size or complexity. To deny the view that even a huge multinational is not a team under the right leadership is clearly ludicrous. There are countless examples of this occurring and it must remain one of the most important objectives of any chief executive. However common sense dictates that within the large team that is the company itself, there can and indeed must be many smaller teams, each with their own objectives and a communality of purpose, each contributing towards the success of the whole organisation.

This chapter is concerned with the situation where you are in a position of leading your team, whatever its size. You might have got there by promotion from within the team itself, or been brought in from outside to run it.

OUTSIDE

We all have personal objectives governing why we work. Mostly these are essentially the need to survive, which in our society means generating income, which we can exchange for whatever our priorities determine we need in the way of accommodation, food, clothes etc.

The organisation, whether a company or public service, also exists to help others survive, either by generating income for shareholders or by providing a service to the community as a whole. To avoid over-complication I will use as my example, a typical company retailing personal computers and software. The objective of any company, simply stated is to make a profit for its shareholders. It is obvious that we must qualify this definition further. In our example we could state: "The objective is to make a profit for the shareholders from selling personal computers and software".

This simple statement can then be segmented further, for example, defining the type of market being targeted, the quality and specific products to be sold, and what value added services such as maintenance and bespoke software are to be offered if any. Also of course we must specify it financially as a target in terms of capital employed.

TEAMS WITHIN TEAMS

Equally obvious is the need for each sub division of an organisation to have its own individual (team) objective. This will usually be a discreet sub-set of the overall corporate objective, concerned mainly with the specific function of the unit but more specialised and detailed.

By taking our computer-retailing example further let us examine the sales team. They would quite correctly, define their mission as selling the company's products and services profitably. They would have financial targets to aim at as well as the ones concerning product mix. Typically the commission scheme would reflect both the sales volume and profitability.

In a highly competitive market the profitability aspect can quickly become clouded with the emphasis shifting to pure volume in an attempt to preserve market share, bulk purchasing discounts, competitive strategy etc. Also members of the sales team will attempt to engineer price reductions calculated to maintain volume, their true motive usually to preserve their individual commission earnings if purely based on volume.

The company may then find itself with the choice of restructuring the commission scheme in an attempt to reverse the downward trend towards unprofitable sales, or to risk losing competent sales professionals in a job market where, whatever the state of the economy and the job market in general, good sales executives are always much in demand. All too quickly a commercial sector looking for a twenty-five percent plus margin can find itself down around six or seven percent.

The sales team will still claim that they are sticking to the objectives they have been set, that of selling the company's products and services. In a way they are doing so. The mistake is they are losing sight of the overall purpose of profitability. This confusion gets particularly problematic when growth of turnover becomes part of the equation.

Many organisations define high growth as an integral part of the main objective, perhaps to obtain a significant market share, ahead of and at the expense of short-term profits. They might be targeting this specific market share, fattening the turnover in order to sell the company or establishing a specialised service prior to improving their margins.

They might need to move certain volumes of specific products to maintain or achieve high discount levels from their own suppliers. There could be many and varied reasons for not maintaining profitable margins. These could change frequently, in some businesses almost on a day-to-day basis.

CONTINUAL CHANGE

It can be seen that it is not such a simple matter therefore to maintain a clear objective, even in a tiny sales team in a small to medium sized company such as a typical personal computer dealer. This at first might seem surprising as most people think they know what they are doing at work, and therefore what their objectives are. However as we can see, the objective, particularly of a team at departmental level may move almost on a daily basis and can, under the continually changing

127

conditions of commercial life, become quite confused and blurred.

It therefore obviously becomes of major importance that the leader of the team devotes sufficient time to maintaining the objectivity of the team, frequently restating them if necessary, and being prepared to redefine them if they are not readily understood. In doing so many practical problems will emerge - these in turn will have an effect on the continual fine tuning of the overall company objectives that is so essential for commercial success.

Remember, business is a process of continual change. Organisations that cannot or will not accept and undertake change soon cease to exist.

MISSION STATEMENT

It has become fashionable in recent years for organisations to have a declared mission statement or company ethos published internally as a staff objective. Hopefully encapsulated in a single sentence, it should be easy to recall and a sentiment that most of the team support and believe in.

Ideally it should not duplicate in any way the main objectives of the company, aiming to clarify or augment them with a philosophy pledging quality of product, excellent service, or integrity in dealings.

Although I fully support the rational behind the establishment of such focal points particularly in such areas as customer service, and indeed frequently have helped set them, I am wary of merely following what is currently trendy. On meeting new contacts I frequently enquire into what is the ethos or mission statement of their organisation. More often than not I receive a blank look of incomprehension in return. Many are employees of companies who 'think' they have a mission statement...

... perhaps they do...

More often than not it has never been effectively communicated to quite senior employees and has certainly not made the overall penetration it should have. If it is not clear enough or inspirational enough to be remembered it certainly will not be taken seriously or respected.

TEAM STATEMENT

There is absolutely no point in having a mission statement if it is not remembered, respected, and acted upon by the bulk of the team members to which it applies. The wrong statement can quickly become a joke an object of ridicule. It is then a negative asset. Most are also forgotten far too easily, particularly after the initial burst of enthusiasm.

Even if the company ethos or mission statement does not exist or is discredited or forgotten, there is no reason why teams within the organisation should not have their own understanding. Perhaps the leader of such a team, particularly if it is not at the 'sharp end' of the business dealing directly with customers or researching high technology, would like to remind team members of the importance they nevertheless play.

All departments contribute to the organisation's overall success. It falls upon the leader of each particular team to continually remind them of their contributions. If developing a particular mission statement will help reinforce the team's detailed objectives then it should be done.

BELIEVABLE AND ACHIEVABLE

In formulating a mission statement it is important to remember to keep it realistic. It is not enough to just invent a slogan that is idealistic and elitist but is too far outside the current capabilities of the team.

By all means hope to be for example, the biggest computer manufacturer in the world, but if you have recently started up the company, you are very unlikely to overtake Apple in the foreseeable and forecast able future. Therefore state something attainable such as "providing the best after sales service in your area of the country". By all means let your ambitions show but in a practical, realistic, and realisable way.

Involve your team in the identification and formulation of the statement. They will believe in it more strongly if they feel they truly originated it. Keep it simple and brief, something everyone can remember easily. It must be something you all can wholeheartedly believe in.

Use it. Keep referring to it until all the team believe in its efficacy. Keep it in the forefront of their minds. Make it work effectively. If you cannot it is probably not worth having.

DEMOCRACY

The only forms of democracy I believe in within a business are the votes of the shareholders. It is after all their company. Their wishes must be paramount. I cannot accept that anyone can be the boss, the real leader of a team, and do it democratically.

The boss is there to make decisions not count votes. A wise leader consults the members of the team who can contribute expertise and opinion relevant to the issue. He or she would be a fool not to do so.

However the team does not make the decision. The leader is there to do that. Sometimes the decision will run completely counter to the unanimous wishes of the team members. So what? That is one of the reasons for having a leader - to take the tough decisions. Using their greater experience and skills to solve the decisions nobody else wants to take responsibility for.

A good leader will of course take counsel from members of the team if time allows and if it is felt they can contribute towards the resolution of the issue. It is after all of vital importance that wherever possible those affected by the outcome feel involved in the process, providing some input to decision making. They will then be much more likely to enthusiastically accept the result and then work towards its success.

CONSENSUS WEAKNESS

The boss who seeks consensus from the team on matters requiring a major decision is a weak leader. It is great when consensus exists because everyone can see the validity of the arguments supporting the proposal but real life situations are not often like that. If the situation were to be so obvious that the best course of action were apparent to everyone, then the problem or issue would not be assuming the proportions necessitating a major decision.

Being a complete autocrat or dictator whilst maybe conforming to a particular 'tough' or 'hard' image is of course too far towards the other extreme. Whilst I insist that the boss must always make the decision even if it is merely to accept the advice of his colleagues, it must in no way be seen as 'taking a vote'.

It is essential that everyone affected feels involved in the decision. The danger in the completely dictatorial approach is that the rest of the team give up, feeling quite   rightly   that they   have   been   excluded from contributing to the decision making process. They then feel free to disassociate themselves from the outcome of the project if it goes wrong, in a way, which it would be far more difficult for then to do if their opinions had been considered before decisions had been made.

DECISION MAKING

In our generally run down industrial and commercial climate most decisions even if they turn out to be the correct ones, are far too long in the making. Normally the reason behind this procrastination is fear- the dread of making the wrong decision.

Such insecurity materialises as over lengthy, over detailed consultation and information gathering prior to taking the decision.

Whilst I do not suggest that decisions should be deliberately made on the basis of incomplete data, I cannot tolerate the tactic of repeatedly asking for more information purely to delay having to 'bite the bullet'. Anyone who has attempted to do business with our Civil Service departments will no doubt recognise this technique carried to an extreme and elaborate art. This is of course unfortunately at the expense of the rest of us in more ways than one.

Basic research on organisational decision-making indicates that the correct decision is just as likely to be made sooner rather than later...

... so why is it not?

There is a significant statistical bias in favour of not delaying decisions. The 'score' of 'right' decisions against wrong ones, shows no significant advantage in delaying them beyond the initial, essential fact gathering. There have been very few prizes for procrastination. The sooner the decision is made, the sooner its benefits are enjoyed.

Be decisive.... gather the essential data rapidly... consult... decide...

... communicate...

Although I strongly argue against a democratic process in decision-making, there are many occasions when you allow others to effectively make the decision. In many instances team members will seek urgent decisions from you although they already know the best course to take. They naturally feel it is not their role or their responsibility to make the decision on their own initiative.

Maybe they are scared to do so or feel that they are not paid for that responsibility. Perhaps they believe that as you are the boss, you should make the decision and take responsibility for it. They perhaps previously have been intimidated into not offering opinions that would affect the situation, possibly by an insecure boss keen on being seen as the one who 'makes the decisions'. Such previous conditioning has a lot going against it when you are trying to develop a deeper sense of responsibility within the team. It is not helpful in cultivating greater involvement, or in assisting individual team members to acquire a greater confidence and understanding in their own abilities.

COUNSELS

When faced with this situation or a variation of it, discuss the problem with the person concerned using your broader experience to explore all the ramifications and alternatives. You will probably quickly see the correct course of action. However ask your colleague what he or she believes to be the best approach. After all they might have more information than you do and could already have formulated a solution, although preferring not to volunteer it. Nine times out of ten their solution will be as good or perhaps even better than yours if it is in the area of their particular specialisation.

If this is the case, thank them, compliment them, and tell them to go ahead with their solution to the problem. Give them full responsibility for carrying it out, and award them the full credit when they succeed. If however there should be a failure, be sure you make it clear that you back them and personally take full responsibility for it being the wrong decision.

Your decision was to back the judgement of your team member which at the time you believed to offer the best solution, therefore you must take the blame if it turns out to be wrong. Give the team member the credit when it proves correct.

When you find you cannot back a proposal or idea from one of your team, the way in which you turn them down is very important. It must always be done by way of an explanation of the reason you made your decision. It must never be purely a simple refusal.

Everyone has feelings, and there is little so depressing as having an idea in which you may have invested much thought, time and effort, rejected out of hand. To do so is not just insulting to a member of your team but it could mean you have overlooked something of value or importance.

Very often those closely involved with a function or project have the best insight into improving the way things are done. They have views and ideas which are always worth considering whatever their status in the organisation. Make sure they are always considered, and that you give full praise and thanks for offering up the suggestion, whatever the outcome.

This way you encourage your team to think for themselves. They are more involved and therefore more motivated. Each team member rapidly gains confidence in his or her own judgement. They appreciate that you are giving them responsibility and that you value their opinion and advice. They believe more in themselves.

RESPECT DOES NOT COME FROM JOB TITLE

Unfortunately there are still many in top jobs 'hiding' behind their job titles thinking their status should guarantee them respect from those lower down the pecking order.

These people surely deserve only the term 'managers', and very poor ones at that. They are in no way, leaders. Such 'respect my job title' individuals also subscribe to outdated symbols and badges of status, helping themselves to privileges that in our modern world can seem faintly absurd.

Although far from my first encounter with this de-motivating phenomenon, my first true realisation of its total divergence from considerations of ability, or contribution to the organisation, materialised in my first computer industry job, when I was aged nineteen. At the time my consuming ambition was to become a computer programmer.

Almost all of the companies I approached rejected me because I lacked any academic qualifications. To program a computer in those far off days, when they were popularly called 'electronic brains' and even a transistor was a rarity, it was generally considered necessary to have a degree in mathematics.

All I could add to my handful of O-levels was my experience as a village postman and a handful of other jobs, none of any particular relevance. My job applications were not very successful. One or two of the more enlightened companies (in recruitment terms at least), used aptitude tests as part of their selection procedure but still predominantly recruited graduates for programming work.

My persistent applications rewarded me with two interviews that included aptitude tests. Being lucky enough to score highly on these tests, both companies offered me jobs. I accepted and joined one of them.

Employed to program on a starting salary of ten pounds per week (£520 per annum), paid weekly. The other programmers were paid £720 per annum, payable monthly. The explanation for the higher salary was that it was the pay scale for university graduates, whilst my lower academic standard qualified me only for a factory worker's pay. This was despite the fact I would be doing the same job as the graduates.

It was interesting that by my early twenties - not only was I several years ahead of the graduates in terms of experience - I was far ahead of them in earning power and had already accumulated useful capital whilst they had lack of funds due to their college years...

... who was the brighter one?

I did not have a problem with that. The graduates were all at least two years older and I accepted that they deserved a little extra for their degrees. The distinctions did not however stop there. As I did not fit the normal programmer profile I could not be classified as 'salaried staff', hence having to be paid weekly instead of monthly.

That was not all. For some reason I never fully understood, I could not be classified as 'office staff' either and was therefore graded as a factory worker. Despite doing the same job and sharing an office with the graduate programmers.

DISCRIMINATION

Then to my increasing amazement other differences emerged. As a 'factory worker' I was supposed to wear a white coat even though I shared the same office and did the same work as others wearing suits. In addition my working hours were 8.00 AM to 5.00 PM, whilst those of my suit attired graduate colleagues scheduled as 9.30 AM to 5.30 PM. On arriving in the morning they had to sign a register kept with the doorman at the main office entrance.

In contrast I had to use the factory entrance, which was an inconvenient four hundred yards from the office in which I worked. At the factory entrance was a mechanical time clock.

If I didn't use it to punch my factory worker time card as I came in through the factory entrance then I did not receive any pay for that day. Every situation however has its bright side. As a factory grade worker I was eligible for paid overtime. The salaried graduates were not.

The discrimination did not stop there. The site had four, yes four, grades of lavatories. One for directors, another for senior managers, a third level for 'ordinary' salaried staff, and of course the most basic and uncomfortable for the factory workers.

You get no prizes for guessing the one I was supposed to use. I never did, preferring the 'ordinary salaried staff lavatory' patronised by my colleagues. We all would, being of anarchist disposition, have used the senior staff one, but its access was restricted to those issued with a special key. The nearest 'factory grade' lavatory was some distance from my office. My 'rebellion' therefore had less to do with anarchy or snobbery, just sheer convenience.

Thus at an early age I learned some fundamental facts about industrial relations in a large and famous British manufacturing company. Operate a class system! Keep the workers in their place! No wonder the company no longer exists as a major manufacturing force and has long since fallen out of computer manufacturing despite having made an excellent product.

There was similar discrimination in the dining facilities. Here my 'factory status' created an even more bizarre situation. Obviously I was supposed to use the factory canteen. Of course normally I ignored this in order to join my colleagues in the staff restaurant. However as my duties often involved training customers, when I was with a customer I had to take them to the senior staff restaurant, or if they were particularly senior, to the director's dining suite. Thus my eating would cover the whole range of the company's dining facilities. No wonder we all needed a sense of humour to work there. Incidentally the best and cheapest food was in the factory canteen, but my graduate colleagues would not eat in there...

... even when I offered to lend them a white coat...

Somewhat irrelevant to the point I am making, except to show that every situation can be exploited by an opportunist, as were the circumstances presented to me by my having to commence work before the others, at 8.00 AM. At the time we all worked on the prototype model of our computer range. A somewhat undistinguished 'lash-up' with almost as many old-fashioned vacuum tube valves as it had transistors. It was used for trying out new ideas and for development, and really was at the forefront of technology at the time - as advanced as anything in the world.

Because computers did not, as the 1950s faded into the swinging '60s, have anywhere near the degree of reliability they have today, exaggerated by the prototype being a development machine with all sorts of novel bits and pieces hung onto it for trial, it required several hours of preventive maintenance each morning. Engineers commenced this work very early and were scheduled to complete it at 10.00 AM, at which time it was handed over to us programmers.

If the work went well and no snags were found, they sometimes handed it over earlier and the computer became available for our use.

This provided me with an opportunity. The graduate programmers scheduled to start work at 9.30 usually arrived late not having to punch an intimidating time clock like me, their 'factory worker' colleague. It was then their habit to hold a competition to see who could complete the Daily Telegraph or Times (I cannot remember which) crossword. This vital and gainful activity nicely filled their time until the tea trolley arrived at 10.30 AM. After the essential tea and doughnut they would be fully fit, fired up ready for anything. Fully physically and mentally prepared to start what they were paid to do by 11.00 AM.

With any luck they could get in a good one and a half hours work before the visit of the tea trolley - on the prototype of Europe's first transistorised computer - one of the worlds most advanced computer at the time.

FREE COMPUTER TIME

Now crossword puzzles are one of the many things I am useless at. However I was determined to become brilliant at computer programming. I hung around the computer room and became friendly with the engineers who like me wore white coats and not suits. Whenever they finished their work ahead of schedule they offered the computer to me.

This was 'free' computer time - to use as I wished. There I was with one of the world's most advanced computers all to myself, and nobody to see what I used it for. Even if they had arrived, my colleagues were far too preoccupied with their crossword competition. With all this extra computer time to use as I wished, I was able to explore the capabilities of the machine and develop my programming skills at a rate far faster than if I had stuck to the rules. Whilst the graduates became experts at crossword puzzles, I started a process that within five or six years was to make me probably one of the best programmers in the world at that time.

My real message of course, is how such antiquated habits and policies of status and privilege survived so recently. Maybe they are still there in places. No wonder we have, as a manufacturing nation, fallen so far behind many other countries.

I often wonder where that long gone computer manufacturer would be now if it had been led with charisma and inspiration, rather than managed in an old fashioned and feudal way.

What would we have achieved if we had been shown a vision of where the computer industry was going to go, and how far we were in the vanguard - we had the product, we had the brains. Did we have the leadership? No one ever asked me my opinion.

Instead of feeling that I was an important member of an exciting team of winners, I was made to feel I was an anomaly and outcast - an uneducated 'factory worker' amongst all those bright graduates. Nobody seemed interested in my ideas or opinions and I was too young and inexperienced to know how to promote them without fear of intellectual ridicule.

Sadly the situation did not apply just to me. We all felt divorced from what the company was trying to achieve. Management made a virtue of keeping as much to itself as it could. Information would gradually grow from rumour into a possible happening, then eventually into fact.

We were hardly ever informed as to what was going on. We drifted back and forth oblivious that the tide carrying us was the most exiting one of the centuries...

... we were not led...

Everyone must be seen and respected for their abilities. They should understand the real contribution they make. The lack of leadership, the status conscious 'class system' operating in that company, provided a breeding ground for jealousy, resentment, potential industrial relation problems.

We were not motivated. We were apathetic towards our commercial destiny. No wonder it has long ceased to exist as a computer manufacturer, having failed to change, to respond to the market, unable to develop its brilliant ideas into usable products. Sadly going the same way as so many of our previously great manufacturing companies.

CONTRAST

Although I had already observed and learned many things that would mould my future attitudes towards the leadership of others in the workplace, my next employer was to provide me with a stark contrast in the treatment of its employees. It was, and not surprisingly still is, a major world force in confectionery manufacturing.

In its offices and factory there was no discrimination. Everyone, from the lowest to the highest had to punch the time clock going in and coming out of the premises. Even the managing director had to take his turn in the queue at 'clocking in time'. The company paid a time-keeping bonus, so courtesy did not enter into it. You gave way to no one when the hand on that clock was one tick away from you 'losing' your ten percent 'time keeping bonus' for the day.

Serving both factory and offices was only a single canteen, a self-service one in which everyone including visitors, fed. It had the reputation of being the best in town and we were justifiably proud of it. No status was accommodated or taken with the lowest paid often sharing tables with the bosses.

Frequently the MD would be seen chatting naturally with someone from the production line with whom he happened to be sharing a table, and no doubt exchanging useful views and information. I bet that many a decision was influenced by information gathered in this way. It also portrayed the MD as an interested and effective communicator - totally approachable. Not frightened of hearing 'grass roots' opinion face to face.

The whole of this company's philosophy was geared to similar status-free policies and actions - a vivid contrast to my previous employer. No wonder the latter one still enjoys its dominant position today.

The company knew precisely where it wanted to go and involved everyone in getting there, both in terms of activities and rewards. We were all immensely proud to work there. Its policies were decades ahead of the field.

I learned much from my comparative experience of both that and my earlier employer. Even now when I almost daily enjoy eating the products of the latter one, I sometimes remember the long-lost computers produced by the former…
… I mourn for what could and should have been…

HIDING BEHIND THE JOB TITLE

Having learned early the effects of discrimination based on status within a company, it was not surprising that I observed many other undesirable aspects of managerial behaviour along side it. The most disturbing aspect from a leadership viewpoint is what I refer to as 'hiding behind the job title'. I believe in showing respect for the person not for their job title.

An idiot is an idiot, irrespective of whether the title is office cleaner or managing director. It is usually much easier however, to communicate with the cleaner than with the managing director.

Many occupants of top positions, who are, often without realising it, incompetent or inadequate in a variety of ways, develop an aversion to meeting members of their teams unless it is almost a 'set-piece' encounter. Finding it uncomfortable or embarrassing to be confronted with surprise problems or situations where they might not have ready a confident answer, their instinct is to avoid the uncomfortable encounter at all costs.

Normally with the help of secretarial staff they will be extremely unavailable, hiding behind a strategy of meeting only by appointment, usually some considerable time in the future. This strategy becomes such a way of life that virtually all meetings, whether they have the potential to pose a problem or not, are subject to a rigid and far-off scheduling. The boss, by putting back the meeting, hopes the problem will go away.

One aspect of being a good team leader is your availability to your team. Their problems are of the highest priority. When I see this obvious strategy of hiding from problems hoping they will disappear, I know that the perpetrator is either inadequate as a leader, or is under so much stress, real or imagined, that a serious lack of leadership exists.

The secretary 'protecting' the boss from the bothersome attentions of team members is often well meaning after all only carrying out instructions. The reality is that the boss is using the status, the title of the job - as a tool to avoid people...
... the boss is in effect hiding behind the job title...

"IT'S COMPANY POLICY"

This particular breed of boss also has another hiding place. One called company policy. It is typically a strategy of the bureaucratic school of management. It offers an easy get out when carrying out a course of action that is challenged by a subordinate.

Justifying an obviously inferior decision on the grounds of company policy can only be upheld in a few short-term situations. Bad policies like bad law attract widespread disrespect and will deteriorate into ridicule.

Where a team leader finds he or she tending towards the upholding of policy that is obviously flawed, the time has come to fight for its replacement by something more in keeping with the organisation's objectives.

OPEN DOORS

The successful highly self-confident leader will always have spare capacity in his or her schedule for meeting team members to discuss unforeseen problems of all kinds. This is the only sensible and realistic course. Even the simplest of enterprise will in the course of time encounter many unforeseen situations...

... nothing ever goes completely as planned...

Some unscheduled meetings will of course be needed. Not necessary for highly visible problems, but maybe a personal problem a team member is seeking advice or counselling for, or they might be having one of those often momentary periods of depression that we all suffer from in the middle of a long project, or a time where nothing new or exiting seems to be happening.

Whatever the nature of the problem it requires immediate attention from the team leader if the best efforts of the team member are to be achieved. If the problem is an emotional one, left alone it could grow out of all proportion.

I do not advocate a totally 'open-door' policy. Those seeking to continually be in the forefront of the boss's awareness, all too easily abuse it. Such 'abuses' of the system can be quite easily discouraged. The important thing is to be accessible to your team members when they really need you.

Few things are worse than being unable to access the boss for a decision or help when you really need it. So obvious and elementary are these commonsense facts that it astonishes me that those in top jobs who hide behind their job titles still survive, but they do.

If you do not 'have time' to listen to a member of your team who needs your help or advice, then you are not a leader in my definition of the word, and are not helping to build loyalty and respect for yourself amongst your team.

LEADING FROM THE FRONT

I must confess to having some very old-fashioned ideas on many areas of leadership. I believe the captain should be the last to abandon the sinking ship, the pilot of the aircraft the last to parachute out, and a general should lead his troops into battle, and not just survey the scene from the hill above, issuing orders but not sharing the risks.

I believe government ministers should resign when proven to be incompetent or even unaware of matters under their charge, and I believe that anyone who benefits from a position in charge of others should be the first to take the responsibility and consequences when things go wrong.

Similar considerations must prevail in our working lives - how can the boss expect respect if he or she always blames staff when things go wrong. How can the boss not also take a salary cut or pay-freeze when the team is expected to do so?

Even as I write this the media is full of reports of 'top bosses' helping themselves to massive, sometimes fifty or sixty per cent pay increases whilst telling their work-forces they can only have a rise in line with the current four or five per cent inflation rate. That is not leadership - it is exploitation and greed. How can they then complain when the same work force treats the words of their bosses with scepticism, disbelief, and often contempt?

Good leaders share the risks and put up with similar conditions to their teams. Obviously they expect to be paid more and to receive perks in line with their additional responsibility, but they know how important it is not to be greedy, not to give the impression they are 'raiding the larder' at the expense of their team.

I believe there was a time when in the finest cavalry regiments the rule followed by the officers was; first attend to the horses, then to the troops, then to themselves…
… it was a good rule...

I have nothing but contempt for bosses who blame their staff when things go wrong, never accepting responsibility themselves, for the shambles and ineptitude over which they preside. Usually they are the ones who are always first to stick their greedy snouts into the financial trough.

Never delegate distasteful tasks because you find them unpleasant. If you have to delegate them, make sure you do so to someone who is in no doubt that you have equally tough jobs to perform. If you have to delegate two tasks, one of which is more unpleasant than the other. Do the nasty one yourself. This is particularly important with something such as a dismissal. It is never pleasant to have to fire someone but some dismissals are bound to be more traumatic than others.

If circumstances permit do not delegate sackings. Even if the person being dismissed is so junior that you would normally not be involved, but for some reason the dismissal interview is likely to be unpleasant, then at least offer to be present. Word will soon get around that you are prepared to do the 'dirty work' yourself, and it will be appreciated and respected.

There are times, fortunately relatively few, when leading from the front will involve you playing for very high stakes, putting not just your job at risk, but your entire career. Maybe even your ability ever to get a top job again.

Consider for example if you are chief executive of a company, itself a subsidiary of a larger group. If, following adverse financial results perhaps for example caused by a deep economic recession, you were directed by the chief executive of your parent company, in effect your owners, to make staff cutbacks that would decimate your key staff, and effectively destroy any chance you had to trade your way out of your difficulties.

Say for example that by obeying the directive you would preserve your own job, but would in reality become little more than a puppet of the holding company.

What would you do? Do you look after your own position, where maybe you have invested twenty years of your working life? Or do you put your own job on the line if your arguments cannot reverse the directive, and you feel you should refuse to carry it out? Would your loyalties lie with the team you had been carefully building and developing, or would self-preservation take over?

Although I am a great subscriber to the survival instinct there are times when we all should stand up and be counted. In my view a real leader will fight like a tiger to keep the team together, obviously applying all the arguments that can be mustered, but in the final count if reason fails, will still 'go down' with the team.

I appreciate that real life is never going to present such a simple case as in my example, and that the financial responsibilities most of us have would impose an almost unbearable pressure on the fictitious leader I portray, but what would you do?

Whatever arguments of personal circumstances, ambition, fear, 'living to fight another day' and other rationalisations are applied, the true leader will put the interest of the team first, fighting to keep them together and if unsuccessful, becoming unemployed with them as a result…

… sometimes even, books are written as a consequence…

In my long business career I have often encountered groups who would be better off without their boss. The boss has needed the group, for without them he or she would have no job. The group however had no need for the boss. In most cases they were a long-established department performing a well-tried and tested function. What decisions were required would be routine and well within the capability of the individual members of the group. We have all probably witnessed similar situations. Our larger companies and institutions are riddled with them.

Why do such groups need a specific leader, a 'manager'? Most of the time this figure simply acts as a pipeline for the work of others, adding nothing of value to it. Not even effectively controlling its quality although claiming 'responsibility' for it. When things go wrong the sub-ordinates are blamed. When the boss is asked to make a decision it is invariably referred 'upstairs'. What is the point of such individuals? They serve no useful purpose, and act as an obstacle to the progress of more able and ambitious people. They are merely figureheads that no one respects.

Fitting easily into the discredited bureaucratic style of management' they are as obsolete and out of date as the dinosaur.

It is unfortunate that so many of these positions still exist. It reflects on the overall leadership of the organisation that has not identified the opportunity to merge such departments with other units, under a single more meaningful, necessary and effective leadership.

A mutual need for each other must exist between team and leader. In the example above such a mutual need does not exist - only the boss's need to have a group to be in charge of. A totally futile reason - the group, to all intent and purpose, would make their own day to day decisions - and in so many examples there exists no ongoing changes, restructuring, or external challenges, requiring a leader's involvement.

Whenever faced with a real problem the boss would refer it upwards. No mutual need exists. The boss is not a leader - that function, is carried out by someone higher in the organisation structure.

We can see that a mutual need is essential if the conditions for leadership are to flourish. It is vital for the leader to realise this. It also means that a strong team needs a strong leader. Where a weak leader is in charge of a strong team the situation will not prevail and the format will eventually change, with a new stronger leader emerging, or the team members gradually drifting away to be replaced by weaker, less able ones.

By the same virtue, quality begets quality. Those good at their job eventually seek the company of similar minds and attitudes...
... the best want to work with the best...

BE SEEN TO GET THINGS DONE

Needed and leading from the front, you should make sure that your efforts are visible to your team. Too much modesty is not a good thing when you are the boss. You are expected to be more capable than most and it should show.

It is especially relevant when you are fighting a battle that will have a major effect on your team's future or their well being, that your efforts are recognised by your colleagues. Even if they can only give you moral support it will provide you with a boost and will enhance the bonding and mutual loyalty within the team.

People love their leader to be a fighter if the effort is directed towards their interests. Be seen to fight...
... be seen to get things done...

ENTHUSIASM FUELS EFFECTIVE TEAM

A good team runs on a fuel of enthusiasm like a racing engine runs on high-octane petrol. When the boss is seen to be getting on with the job it is much easier to keep up a high level of momentum and energy. Again be seen to be leading from the front. That old saying 'actions speak louder than words' is as valid now as it ever was.

Continually encourage involvement and ideas. Even when unworkable or unsuitable ideas are proposed, give time to their consideration and discussion. Never treat anyone in a patronising manner when they are attempting to please you with suggestions and ideas however inappropriate. Deliberately encourage 'wild thinking'. That is how lateral thinking can be cultivated and stimulated. Some of the most unlikely ideas and suggestions have blossomed into major products when bounced around in a 'think-tank' environment.

Be sure to praise the act, the initiative of coming forward with the idea, even if the idea itself is not useful. Never dismiss an idea out of hand. Always find time to explore its feasibility with the person suggesting it, making sure that they see for themselves why you are unable to take it further. This is an essential process. Anything less will be seen as a dismissive rejection, and as well as causing disappointment and frustration, will probably stem the flow of further ideas from the source and possibly from the team as a whole.

Make sure you are seen to be interested in your team. Serious consideration of their proposals is vital in this respect. If you need time to consider an idea or suggestion, state when you expect to have completed your thinking. Arrange a definite date when you will meet your colleague to appraise it further.

Follow your initial meeting up with a note of thanks, together with confirmation that you will meet again to discuss your considered reactions at the agreed date. If you require them to provide any further information or do more work on the idea, also confirm it in your note. This helps convey the message that you have taken their proposal seriously and are yourself committing time to it. Confirm the time and the date of the follow-up meeting...

... on no account forget them...

QUICK TO PRAISE - SLOW TO CONDEMN

When considering the ideas and the proposals of others, be wary of any possible attempt to manipulate you. It is only human nature for members of your team to attempt to influence you in order to advance some real or imagined cause they might have.

Whilst it is often important to be flexible and receptive to other people's ideas, and not dogmatically insistent regarding your own ones, you must not confuse being flexible with being manipulated. Flexibility will be respected and increase team bonding whilst being manipulated will only bring you contempt.

If you are forced to compromise on some issue or other, be sure that everyone concerned and your team in particular, see clearly your reasons for doing so. Most compromises are the result of poor negotiation, lack of resolve, or inability to communicate your true position. Such reasons are weaknesses. When a compromise reflects the best solution and not merely the result of some impasse it should be shown as such. Anything else smacks of a fudged decision.

AVOID THE 'STATUS GAME'

It is pleasant to enjoy many of the material perks of a top job. Well-balanced and sorted-out team colleagues do not resent these. They look forward to when they too will enjoy similar rewards, and take pride in an organisation that is doing well enough to give its top people the best. Some bosses take perks of different kind, namely behavioural ones. Acting in a way that indicates they are in a class above their colleagues.

The type of behaviour in this category is a wasteful and needless demonstration of their status - games such as always summoning others to come to the boss's office…
… a territorial game - a sure indication of insecurity…

154

If you wish to discuss something, and it is not ultra confidential, make a habit of going to see team members at their own work-stations unheralded. Why try to intimidate a member of your own team with territorial games, and keeping them waiting outside your office just to reinforce the point that you are the boss?

Remember you are nothing without a good team around you. Do not insult them by reminding them of your seniority in unnecessary ways. Attempt the reverse. I would always vacate my office and make it available to a colleague if they considered it the best place for an meeting with a client or supplier, or needed privacy to conduct an interview or review meeting. Very often they themselves shared an office, and our conference rooms might be too large and impersonal for the size of meeting scheduled.

If I was either out of the building or could easily swap offices for an hour or so, then so much the better. We all worked together. Many were the occasion when I would lend my company car to a member of my team for a client visit or other journey. It was necessary to be selective in this, not on the grounds of status but the need for safety, as I had a penchant for driving Lotus Esprits and some of my staff fancied their potential as racing drivers.

The services of my secretary were always available to all, sales, then production, generally taking priority over finance and administration. Normally she decided the priority. My own work was not necessarily processed first. There are many and varied ways in which the boss can actually play down his or her status rather than continually reminding others of it.

Too many people use status symbols as a substitute for true self-confidence. Those who have the real thing have no need to do so.

COMMUNICATE-COMMUNICATE-COMMUNICATE

Always let your team know exactly where you stand on the issues currently affecting them. Make simple straightforward statements of what you mean. State what the standards of work are to be, the behaviour you expect and the part you want each individual to play. Always make sure the priorities you establish are crystal clear.

It is altogether far too easy to have a meeting or a discussion on an important topic, ending with each participant leaving the meeting with a different interpretation of what has been agreed, differing notions of what is expected. This frequently occurs when sensitive or potentially disruptive subjects are at issue, and the meeting has been vague or 'woolly' skirting around the more controversial points.

Obviously the meeting should have been controlled more specifically and objectively in the first place. However if you feel there was any ambiguity you should remedy the situation immediately. In general I am not a fan of producing large volumes of internal paper whatever the organisation.

Emails to the staff are much more likely to be read if they appear infrequently. There are often more effective ways to communicate, but some things need to be put onto a permanent record.

Very short precise emails to summarise an agreement or to record a schedule are in this category. It is essential of course, always to follow up every agreed date and deadline and to have a reputation for doing so. It will be seen as a reflection of your own efficiency as well as a reminder to the others.

Whilst on the subject of internal communication we should briefly contemplate the email. This is a tool in trade of the bureaucrat and has replaced the traditional memo. For many decades the volume of memos written was one of the productivity measurements of the bureaucratic dinosaur.

For someone of that inclination, emails are a wonderful technique. They can serve as a device to hide behind, avoiding potentially embarrassing confrontational face-to-face meetings - particularly useful when conveying an unpopular edict.

As well as this use as a shield, the email exponent can set up a 'dialogue', sending, receiving, and sending yet more on the same subject seeking clarification on some minor point or other. Endlessly protracting some issue until everyone else gives up from sheer exhaustion or frustration.

Because I have watched with a measure of contempt, too many of these bureaucratic strategies, I have perhaps gone too far in the other direction, not committing enough to paper.

Whenever you do communicate, always be sure you have been understood. Remember always you are dealing with individuals. Some will understand you better at times than at others. Sometimes you will barely be understood at all. Gently test to check that what you meant is what has been understood.

As in everything else get regular feedback from your team.

Whenever you delegate, you must stay involved in some way. Never delegate a task or project then just walk away from it. That would be abdicating your responsibility, which is not what you are there for.

Always maintain an ongoing interest so that you can keep a regular check on the proceedings without appearing to pry or to interfere...

... delegate, but stay interested...

KEY POINTS

* A team or merely a group of people?
* Chief Executive - smart name for overall team leader
* Without continual change a company will eventually die
* A good mission statement reinforces the team's objectives
* As Chief Executive - democracy is only for the shareholders
* The leader is there to make decisions - not to count votes
* Insecurity shows when fear delays and inhibits decisions
* Before making difficult decisions, listen to relevant team members - they are the specialists
* Always give credit where due to others - you take the blame but not the glory
* Rejection of someone's ideas can hurt them - always give full reasons
* Encourage the team to think for themselves- involvement creates motivation and boosts theirself-confidence
* Senior job title not ticket to instant respect - earn it by visible leadership
* Respond quickly to team problems - or they grow out of all proportion
* Leader takes responsibility for all that goes wrong - he or she allowed it to happen
* What is good for your staff is good for you - be it canteen or pay cut
* Best leaders put team first - their job or career on the line if necessary

* Teams love their leader to fight for them - don't be a passenger - get things done
* Enthusiasm - the fuel of an effective team - provide plenty
* Status symbols are no substitute for true self-confidence
* Communicate openly, don't be secretive, and don't play games- be honest and straightforward

SEVEN
Face To Face

Much of the leader's time is, or at least should be spent in close contact with members of the team. The success of what is often a close personal relationship will of course have a major effect on the outcome of the enterprise. As in any close or relatively close relationship, emotions, personality traits and ability to handle the inevitable stress will all have their part to play.

WE ALL NEED EACH OTHER

The very concept of a team suggests mutual dependence. A leader with a poor team might succeed as a leader in terms of relative achievement but could still fail abysmally in meeting the team objectives.

The psychology of the human animal is highly complex, and probably not yet fully understood despite the tens of thousands of books that have been written on the subject. It is not my intention, desire, or indeed my specialisation, to attempt to duplicate them. However over the years I have experienced most behavioural patterns that affect our work performance.

The boss's emotional behaviour, and the way his or her responses are triggered or modified by the normal human feelings are of vital importance as they are easily transmitted to the rest of the team. Obviously transmission of positive emotions such as enthusiasm can have enormous benefits, whilst communicating depression can 'bring down' other members of the team.

161

CAREFUL EXERCISE OF POWER

Remember as the boss you are exercising some form of power over your staff. Whatever this level of control is, its effects on them can be profound. Apart from the obvious influence on the livelihood of others through your power to promote, direct and dismiss, the effect on the emotional health of a team member can also be dramatic.

Many mental illnesses originate at, or are aggravated by a person's job. It is common that the stress caused, not necessarily by problems at work, but by sheer volume or pressure, or by the weight of responsibility, can cause or contribute to cardiac and hypertension problems that could kill. People become ill and indeed die, from problems stemming from their jobs.

It is essential that as the leader of your team you are aware of the effect you could have on the well being of other human beings. A good leader has to be good at analysing what the members of the team feel and has to be highly aware and flexible when dealing at the individual level.

We all need each other in any team - although the old cliché that the boss is only as good as his staff remains as true as ever. Any team will still produce greater results if better led, however good or bad the basic material.

When all is said and done work is merely a transaction. Unless we are independently wealthy we exchange our labours for the means of survival, "to keep ourselves and our families alive, healthy, and as prosperous as possible". Our jobs are our latter-day equivalent of having to leave our mud hut or cave and venture forth to hunt, or to fish - or to find other food forms in a perhaps dangerous environment. To a greater or a lesser extent, we look in our work for substitutes to the natural dangers and confrontations we would encounter in a hunter-gatherer society.

We all retain many of these primitive instincts and needs to some lesser or greater extent. Deprived of the opportunity to kill a bear or fight off a rival tribe many of us look for substitute excitement in the work place. Atavistic instincts are alive and well, even on the threshold of the twenty-first century.

All business is warfare, a battle against competitors, a campaign against the hostile elements represented by the overall economic climate and international considerations way beyond the control or influence of any organisation however large.

The entire the drama of the jungle can be found in business - an ever-changing interaction between creatures on the ascendancy and those on the way down. It is an eternal struggle for supremacy. When we leave home for work we are in effect, in our hereditary subconscious, going forth to hunt or to fight.

ALL INDIVIDUALS

I deeply believe that no two people are truly the same. Everyone is unique in terms of his or her overall pattern of characteristics. The leader must make an effort to understand the particular beliefs and motivations of each team member. Something of great importance to one team member might have little significance to another. You must treat each person you deal with as a separate case. It is of course very difficult and time consuming to do this but it pays dividends when each team member feels that you understand them well.

A face-to-face meeting is obviously the most important method of communication between leader and team for both parties. It is in face-to-face communication that the self-confidence of the boss, or the lack of it, will be at its most evident. Many people become very uncomfortable in the presence of someone who is making considerable demands on them in some way.

Obviously there will be meetings that are extremely pleasant, where you and your team member are mainly in agreement, but there will also be many, which are tense or even highly confrontational. It is when faced with a possible confrontation that some bosses try to hide behind their secretary or personal assistant, and resort to delaying tactics, hoping the problem will go away.

FEAR OF LOSING FACE

One of the most frequent causes of the leader of the team fearing a confrontational meeting is the possibility of 'losing face'. In some societies, mostly in the Middle and Far East, the social stigma caused by loss of face is considered very serious. Fortunately we tend not to take such matters quite so far but for some individuals, usually the more insecure, it still matters a lot.

Loss of face is in reality, an implied loss of honour. When it is the result of, for example, admitting to having made a mistake or a bad decision, it can assume a significance way out of proportion to its true importance.

I have witnessed many 'mature' individuals stubbornly refuse to change their minds on quite trivial matters when they see it as an admission of a mistake, a 'climbing down'. When the issue is of great importance this can become a serious flaw. No one deserves respect when they can and will not admit when they are wrong.

The best leaders will always readily admit it when they are proved wrong. However they will often use the situation to positive gain. Sometimes it can be used to boost the self-esteem of other team members that were involved in recognising or correcting the mistake.

It can also be used to demonstrate 'that the boss is only human after all and not infallible', often arousing a greater degree of respect, and sometimes even sympathy and affection from the team. This can often be turned to advantage and used to the benefit of morale and togetherness.

Never mind about losing face. There are far more significant things to be anxious about if you are the worrying kind. Leave loss of face to those whose system of social honour demands it. A good leader is the first to recognise and admit a mistake. That is part of the combination of decisive quick thinking and honesty that contributes to their leadership qualifications.

CONTROLLING YOUR EMOTIONS

Because when leading a team we can so readily affect the mood of our colleagues the ideal leader would have total emotional control, conveying only intended moods to others. With experience and a great deal of self-control it is certainly possible to go a long way towards this ideal. In fact it is not good to be seen as someone who is too 'emotionally dead'.

165

In the same way that the boss needs to be seen as having normal human frailties by occasionally making a mistake, the same principle also applies to human sensitivity.

It does not pay to be prone to extremes of emotion. In particular anger should always be controlled allowing it to be released in measured amounts. In short if you have a 'temper' you should discipline yourself to control it. It is not clever to be able to use a position of power to indulge in a fit of ranting abuse, when things go wrong, or when someone annoys you.

By all means establish a reputation as someone capable of forceful articulate expression in order to convey your concern, disgust and annoyance, when something has been done badly. However the bigger the mistake, the greater the disaster, the more controlled and cooler your response should be.

When you are seen to be angry it should be a calculated act, used to a specific purpose. Uncontrolled anger shows you are not in control of the situation…
… you must always be in control of yourself…

ICE-MAN

My 'training' in handling emergencies was greatly improved by several incidents I experienced whilst piloting aircraft. Panic, or indeed any sort of emotional reaction other than a short sharp expletive, have no place when your one and only engine fails and you are looking for a field in which to put it down. Or when you suddenly realise the black spots before your eyes half-way across the English Channel, are in fact rapidly multiplying blobs of oil on the windscreen.

Unlike a car, where you can pull to the side and call the AA or RAC - in an aircraft you cannot just stop, you have to try and land somewhere, even if it is a 'controlled crash' into the sea. Such situations have a great way of concentrating the mind. The adrenalin flow hypes your brain into amazing clarity, racing ahead with such speed that one's physical actions appear almost in slow motion.

After 'enjoying' several of these experiences, one of them culminating in the complete write-off of my aircraft I was in danger of becoming complacent. Having dealt with a few occurrences of this nature I soon learned to show an external icy coolness in typical business 'emergencies'.

It is of obvious vital importance that the leader exhibits an icy coolness when faced with a major problem or emergency. That is what is, quite rightly, demanded from him or her. An emergency is never the time to display your human emotions. Be an iceman.

Show you are a sensitive human being by occasionally deliberately displaying your anger at the lesser irritations - preferably on external problems that are not the responsibility of your team. Use your emotional control to release just the 'right' amount of feelings when they will support in some way the common team objective...
... take it out on the opposition, not your own side...

NO EMOTIONAL DECISIONS

Never, ever, make an important decision when your emotions are high - even if the reason for your state has nothing to do with the particular issue in question. Where as the adrenalin secreted in life-threatening physical emergencies heightens senses and aids clear fast thinking, the effects of being in a severe emotional condition can have the reverse effect.

Anger, sorrow and delirious happiness, distort and corrupt one's judgement, biasing it towards the type of emotion being felt. If for example you are extremely angry, although you might not be in a position to affect the cause or object of your anger, an unrelated perhaps quite important issue could receive the full flow of your fury. Many a request for an extended lunch hour has been denied because the boss had a row at home that morning.

If expediency dictates that a decision has to be taken under such circumstances, be aware of the effect your emotional condition could be having on your judgement. Compensate for it. If necessary give yourself a little extra time for some quiet reflection of the problem with particular emphasis on achieving a balanced viewpoint. When emotion could affect your judgement coolly and deliberately make yourself that little extra 'space'.

When you are particularly happy there is a tendency towards making decisions that are over-generous to another party. It might suit a member of your team to benefit from an over-large pay increase because you have just been nominated for a Knighthood, but it would not be conducive to your company's profit when the word gets around and everyone expects similar treatment.

Equally when feeling depressed your decision-making capability will tend to bias towards a negative 'couldn't care less' attitude that could result in a degree of recklessness creeping into your judgement.

Although it is not quite so easy to infect your team with any of the particular happiness or joy of living that you might feel at the time, the reverse is true if you are for any reason in a foul mood.

It is all too easy, after the proverbial row with your wife or your husband before leaving for work, or perhaps a cancelled train or endless traffic jams, to take the resulting frustration and anger with you into the office.

Such a mood is not just infectious. You are more than likely to behave in a snappy and irritable way, conveying your negative vibrations to the others, making them less happy and almost certainly less effective.

Try to keep your personal moods and problems to yourself. Apart from avoiding the effect they could have on the others, it will give you a certain moral advantage when you take to task members of the team for inflicting their own bad moods on colleagues.

One exception to this is when you are suffering from a stress situation. By discussing it with one or more members of your team, you can often clarify the extent of the problems, with the result that they become more manageable.

DEALING WITH STRESS

We all have differing levels of tolerance in our ability to cope with stressful situations. Not surprisingly our stress tolerance will change on a day-to-day basis, sometimes from hour to hour. Your ability to withstand stress is affected by such factors as to how well you are feeling at that moment in time, your current emotional state, and your confidence level.

Your stress tolerance can be easily de-stabilised by normal everyday occurrences such as your train being very late, a nasty letter from your bank, or arriving at the newsagent and finding your favourite magazine has been sold out.

Such minor occurrences can then elevate a routine problem such as a key member of your team resigning, into a situation causing you to uncharacteristically over-react. You might for example, accuse him or her of disloyalty, perhaps sabotaging the project, and insist they leave immediately, despite their willingness to stay on to finish what they are working upon.

This behaviour would of course be in stark contrast to your normal calm, cool, considered reaction to such a problem. It could unfortunately lead you to miss an important signal or 'cry for help' from a colleague.

A resignation is often just this - someone who does not really want to go, but feels that it is the only remaining way to draw attention to their situation. If you miss such a signal due to your own overstressed condition you are greatly compounding the overall problem. In turn your own and everyone else's stress level will increase…
… not a good scene…

The first step towards coping with stress is to recognise that you are actually being affected by it. Normally you will be the last person to realise that you are showing signs of stressful behaviour, although it will be very apparent to those around you from your responses, attitude, your refusal to comply with simple reasonable requests.

If accused of being under stress you will almost certainly initially deny it - maybe quite vehemently. All the while your behaviour and bad vibrations will be causing the stress level to rise in the others around you. In turn this will feed back to you creating a vicious circle.

STRESS RECOGNITION

Try to recognise when you are under stress in any way. Be aware if you are irritated by trivial occurrences. If you find you are almost irrationally objecting to doing simple everyday things like returning a telephone call or signing a cheque, causing inconvenience to your secretary or other colleagues, then these are all indicators that you might be mildly and probably temporarily, suffering from stress and should therefore do something about it.

There are many well-known causes of stress, some of which we are all likely to experience throughout the course of our working and personal lives. Some are surprising, such as a relatively minor car accident, even one where no injury occurs.

Other stress generators that can be predicted at some stage of one's working lives are moving office, promotion, change of company ownership, change of boss, loss of key staff member, and many more. Add to such routine career occurrences some of the less predictable events such as redundancies (either experienced or generated), severe business set-backs, relocation overseas, or a hostile takeover, and it can be seen that every business career will be punctuated by at least some of these well known periods of stress.

Add to the business stresses those occurring during one's private life, and there again getting married (or divorced), moving house, family bereavement, financial problems etc., are all accepted stress generators for most of us, and it can be seen that we all must learn to come to terms with it, and cope with it as a normal, predictable part of our lives if we are to function at our best in the leadership role.

You must try to locate the underlying cause of the stress. The trivial causes of the current 'attack' of stress are obviously not the real reasons for your behaviour, but merely convenient triggers for it to show itself. Stress is seldom caused by a single factor, but by a combination of events having a cumulative effect. Things you have dealt with, rather by things you know, subconsciously perhaps, that you must deal with, never cause it. If you are one of those who tend or try, to put off tackling unpleasant or difficult tasks, you are opening the door to potential stress problems.

When recognising that you are probably suffering from some form of stress you should enter a deliberate and conscious routine to reduce its effect. First of all it is essential to give yourself some time. Sit with a coffee for fifteen minutes making a list of all the things you need to do, major and minor.

Try to delegate as much of the tasks on the list as can be sensibly done including the personal ones. If for example you were trying to find time in the day to do some shopping, and your secretary or personal assistant could do it for you, then explain why they could help reduce your current load by helping you do it.

Positively ask for help, do not treat your secretary like a servant. Good secretaries know when their bosses need such services to allow them time on other matters, as distinct from just laziness. Having reduced your list to the items that you alone can tackle, ruthlessly prioritise them. Even you can only do so much in one day.

By now things should be getting back into proportion and you should be feeling much more confidant about tackling them. Your confident and logical way of calming yourself down and dealing with the situation will then communicate itself to those around you, and your whole team will be in a more positive mood to tackle problems.

Beware of diagnosing stress in yourself when you are only in reality just under pressure. They are very different situations. Stress can cause quite severe depression and if not quickly countered will have a cumulative effect that can get out of control. Pressure can have a reverse, almost stimulating effect, triggering off intensive action.

Unfortunately, as with some other 'illnesses', stress has become fashionable in certain quarters, seen as the badge of the high-powered executive. It a basically a very simple and straightforward condition, that you can well control yourself with a little care and common sense.

COMMON GROUND - COMMON INTEREST

As the leader of the team you are in a position to influence their attitudes to most aspects of their work. Although you are all 'in the same boat', hopefully working towards the team's shared objectives, the clarity with which you perhaps see such things will often become obscured in the eyes of some of your team members for a variety of reasons.

However much we pay lip service to the team approach, there remain occasions when personal ambition, greed, stubbornness, arrogance and many other factors get in the way of the ideal.

Whenever more than two people form a group to undertake some endeavour or to pursue a common interest, then some form of interpersonal politics will occur. Organisations tend to be riddled with politics. Many executives spend more of their time seeking to influence the course of events to their personal advantage, rather than to the company's.

Sometimes involvement in corporate politics may seem a much more interesting way to spend time than getting on with the job, and exponents of the art might feel they are furthering their careers by such manipulation. Beware; it is totally unproductive in the long term as it is a danger to the company.

I assume you employ staff to work not to indulge in manipulative intrigue and debate. If people feel that they have sufficient spare mental energy for such pursuits, the immediate conclusion must be that they are either working below capacity, employed in a position far beneath their intellectual level, or just plain bored or mischievous.

It could be an indicator that someone is in the wrong slot and has talents that could be more productively utilised elsewhere, either within or outside your organisation. Whatever the reasons the resulting disruption is unlikely to be in your long-term interests.

Corporate politics are a disease, a cancer that if left unchecked will eat away at morale and sap individual energy from its correct employment. You will never stamp it out completely but you should be continually vigilant in identifying it and diluting its effects.

Continually emphasise that the mental energy that goes into involvement in corporate politics, is better put to beating the stuffing out of the external competition faced by the company. That is what you expect to see. It is an area where you can afford to be intolerant, and indeed should be. The common interest is the team objective. You should always communicate that message loud and clear, particularly when the issue involves company politics.

FREQUENT APPRAISALS

Obviously people must be expected to do their best to promote their own interests, and you as the boss will spend some time in discussions, both resulting from scheduled appraisals, as well as impromptu conversations arising at other times.

There will always be an on-going dialogue over a multitude of subjects, and only a fool would hope for mutual agreement for most or all of the time. Again the need to treat everyone as a unique individual applies, but there are several important, though again mainly common sense guidelines that apply.

If you know, feel, or anticipate that you will be approached with a specific problem that relates to a particular individual, consider the timing of your meeting. Obviously some things are so urgent or need immediate attention to diffuse a potentially worsening situation, that there is no room for anything other than instant action.

Many other situations however will benefit from a deliberate 'cooling off period. We all have experience of these.

Unfortunately they are often the ones where considerable personal pride or loss of face is at stake. It might therefore require skilful diplomacy and tact to engineer this cooling off, but if it can be done it usually pays dividends. Obviously anything so urgent it requires an immediate decision does not come into this category.

Where possible choose your moment to address the problem when the signs are conducive to the most favourable outcome. Be conscious of what you are trying to achieve, otherwise you will be guilty of merely   procrastinating.

Expect members of your team to also 'choose their moment' when approaching you. If they are sensible that is! Working closely with you they inevitably develop sensitivity to your views and your moods, which give them an insight into when you are most approachable on a specific issue. This is part of the process we all 'manage' each other. Do not be concerned if members of your team attempt to manage you in this fashion...
… it is good involvement and does no harm at all…

NEVER FORCE OTHERS INTO A CORNER

When dealing with others, be very sensitive to the position they are in, particularly any position you may force them into. Any animal that is backed into a corner has only one way to go, and therefore its options are limited.

Always leave others with some room for manoeuvre. Allow them the dignity of some choice wherever possible. Where this is not really feasible, present the result in such a way that the other party's dignity is preserved. It should usually be possible to involve him or her in such a way that they feel part of the decision and therefore in support of it, rather than having an unpopular solution forced upon them.

PRIDE AND DIGNITY

By taking care to treat others in a way that preserves their pride and dignity, you are far more likely to get their full support than if you ride roughshod over them. As the boss you will inevitably have to take many unpopular decisions, some of them affecting your team in a financial as well as a professional way.

Your sensitivity in arriving at these decisions and in implementing them will have a direct bearing on their success, as well as the loyalty you will continue to enjoy from your team.

PRAISE AND CRITICISM

An obvious area where your tact and respect for the pride and dignity of others assumes paramount importance is in the communication of both praise and criticism.

The public commendation of a task well done, can, by its open nature, enhance its value to the recipient. We all take pride in achievement but it is not so enjoyable if others do not witness their recognition. Some public acclaim skilfully applied is an obvious morale booster.

The reverse of course applies to criticism and sanction. Any act of reprimand must obviously be carried out in private to be most effective. To do otherwise, shows a serious lack of respect for the team member concerned, which might win you points in the undesirable game of 'point scoring', but will on close analysis expose your own insecurities and perhaps an unhealthy need to humiliate people who you have power over, and who you are supposedly supplying leadership to.

Any short term benefit you might think you derive, will be more than paid for in long term loss of respect.

Keep it private. In any group of people who have to spend a length of time together, there will always be a degree of competitiveness. This is often friendly but can of course translate into bitter and serious rivalry. Whilst this is inevitable, it is also to a certain extent desirable.

Competition is the author of endeavour and progress. We need it to bring out the best within us. However as the boss, you should not need to compete with your team on the same level. You are already ahead of them and should aim to stay ahead by you performance as leader, not by doing the jobs of others for them.

It is therefore unnecessary to compete with your team even on a 'social' level. Avoid any situation, action or remark that could be interpreted as a competitive point-scoring exercise. Aim all that at the team or the company's competitors. Be careful not to appear to be 'playing games' with your colleagues. Do not waste their time on tasks that they might consider unnecessary. Make sure they always know the reason for doing something. Do not tease them on serious matters.

Above all do not play one off against another. Be aware if team members are playing the same unproductive games with each other.

Treat such practices in the same way as you handle team members indulging in corporate politics. They are equally a waste of valuable physical and mental energies that are best channelled into beating the company's competitors. Remember you and your team are all on the same side.

KEY POINTS

* As team leader you transmit moods to others - make sure they are always positive
* Effort taken to understand personal motivation amongst team is time well spent
* Self-confidence is most evident in face-to-face meetings
* Fear of confrontation caused by possibility of 'losing face'
* Best leaders always ready to admit when they are wrong
* Showing 'human feelings' can often strengthen your relations with your team
* Leader should be known as a forceful articulate communicator - not someone with a foul temper
* You can indulge your irritability over the small things - over the big ones, be an Ice Man
* Very angry, very sad, or very happy - not the time to make important decisions
* Learn to recognise a potential stress situation before it occurs
* Open discussion often diffuses high stress levels
* Beware of transmitting your stress to others
* You can't do everything yourself
* Know the difference between stress and pressure
* Corporate politics are cancer
* Boredom causes mischief and manipulation - keep team members working to their full intellectual capacity
* Don't fence people into a corner - leave a little room for manoeuvre
* Respect the pride of others
* Competition is the author of endeavour - but don't compete with those working for you

EIGHT
Recruiting

As you spend time in the leadership role there will be a reoccurring pattern of activities that have to be mastered as part of your successful career. Several of the topics have been discussed briefly in earlier chapters, but are of sufficient importance to require covering in greater depth.

It is beyond the scope of this book to go into specialised professional disciplines such as financial control or marketing. I will continue to confine my comments to the personal qualities encompassed in good leadership without deviating too much into specialist roles. It is about being in charge and does not matter too much what manner of team is being led...
... the principles remain the same...

THE IMPORTANCE OF RECRUITING

As the boss your success is largely dependent on the abilities of your team. It is therefore obvious that when extending and replacing elements of the team, you must obtain the best people for the positions being filled.

Most people in top jobs will tell you that they always recruit the best candidates available. This is just not true. Many in leadership positions are lousy recruiters, whilst others deliberately do not recruit the most able, fearing the competition it might bring about.

Almost everyone over-delegates the recruitment process. This over-delegation, much of it to external agencies, is especially corrosive, as the more people in the recruitment chain the more filtering of the best candidates, due to the personal prejudices, complexes, and 'political' ambitions of those in the chain.

The more people involved in the recruitment process the more likely it is that the 'successful' candidate will be a mediocre compromise.

RECRUITING - ONE OF THE MOST IMPORTANT JOBS YOU DO

The importance of the recruiting process cannot be overemphasised, neither can be the consequent dangers of over-delegating it. It is one of the areas where delegation is least appropriate, yet it remains perhaps the area where most delegation takes place. This is very curious. Having spent much time examining why this should be so, I can only conclude that it is all about not wanting to take responsibility.

But why should the boss be so reluctant to take more responsibility for recruiting? Why set up a typical chain of delegation through the personnel, sorry, human resources department, recruitment consultant or head-hunter? Why from perhaps several hundred candidates applying for the position, see only details of a short list of five or six? A short list selected expensively, and at length, by people you certainly would not allow to choose your suit, shirt, or necktie...
… curious is it not?

OVER-DELEGATION

Recruiting is too important to delegate! It requires the best judgement available. This judgement should come from the person who stands to lose or gain the most by the success or failure of the recruitment project. That person has to be the team leader. You do not delegate your future.

Over-delegation of the recruitment process is literally delegating a slice of your future. Forget all the arguments about not having the time etc.

For recruitment, particularly of key team members, you make the time available. Anything else smacks of lack of confidence, unwillingness to take full responsibility for the choice, or indicates your own inability to select.

Obviously I am not referring to categories of staff so junior you would not have time to handle the volume.

Whatever your reasons for not being deeply involved and taking full responsibility, it represents a sad and to me unacceptable side stepping of an essential leadership function.

Consider the processes involved in recruiting and selection. First of all, following the decision to fill a vacancy, replace an existing employee, or fill a newly identified position, a specification of what qualifications and qualities you are seeking must be made.

Contact must then be established with the potential candidates through advertising or by using an agency. CVs have to be reviewed and interviews carried out.

A whole industry has emerged to undertake almost all of the process. In some quarters it has become automatic to use the services of the recruitment industry without any real examination of its effectiveness both in terms of cost, timescale and quality.

Nailing my flag to the mast, I maintain that most companies take far too long to recruit staff, spend much too much on the process, and generally end up getting mediocre employees. It is at best a sloppy waste of resources, at worst a betrayal of your existing team and a sabotage of their future. It is not good leadership!

The almost universal dependency on external recruitment services has of course its origins in a acknowledgement for specialised help. This is of course valid when knowledge of perhaps a technical subject does not exist in the organisation needing the staff.

The group of companies I ran included a recruitment consultancy of which I was the founder. Therefore I cannot be accused of being obsessively anti the recruitment industry. However Computer Personnel International was conceived at a time when computing was so relatively rare and specialised that many companies did not themselves have the detailed knowledge to conduct the technical side of the interview.

A VERY BAD HABIT

There will always be situations where help from experts in a specialised field is justified. The fact of the matter is that most recruitment situations have lost sight of that as the criteria, and the agency, search consultant, head-hunter or whatever you choose to name them, are called in as a matter of course.

Using external recruiting services has for most organisations now just become a habit and a bad one at that.

Technical specialisation is one thing, but it is not acceptable to include the personal qualities sought for in a recruit, as a specialised subject justifying external advice. That would be not just delegating responsibility, but abdicating the very judgement you are paid to exercise.

I know many who do just this but that does not make it right. Sometimes the reason for using external consultants is not just shirking responsibility, but can be a political strategy when there is a strong internal candidate for the position who the boss does not want to get it.

Using an outside consultant suitably briefed is used as a tactic to avoid personal responsibility by attributing the decision to the hired help.

Consultants are also sometimes engaged to filter out categories that reflect the racial, sexist, or ageist prejudices of the employer, a buffer against potential embarrassment. It is a form of cowardice by the boss.

It has also become very fashionable to use so-called scientific and other recruitment aids. As mentioned earlier in this book an entire industry has emerged, from management psychologists, 'experts' in assertiveness training, public speaking, and advice on virtually every aspect of your job.

Amongst these, and very much in vogue, are the personality profiling techniques, psychometric tests, handwriting analysis, aptitude tests, and all the pseudo-scientific mumbo-jumbo uttering expensive 'experts' queuing to take your company's money.

CHANCE

Most of the techniques such as psychometrics and handwriting tests have very little proof of success when measured using accepted statistical methods. The handwriting tests in particular are no more use than tossing a coin to determine a candidate's suitability.

At this stage I was going to jokingly suggest that the next great breakthrough in specialist recruitment advice would be astrology. Events unfortunately have overtaken me. I am reliably informed that this would not longer be considered funny as it is now quite commonly used to aid recruitment in the USA.

Perhaps now there will be an opening for a reader of tealeaves or even the palms of hands. I am sure the success ratio would be no different.

Make yourself responsible for the recruitment of key personnel. You should already have defined the job specification, so writing the advertisement is just as easy as instructing someone else to do it.

If you feel your writing is not up to the 'copy writing' standards of the professionals, and more especially if you need some art-work, then these are readily available from an advertising agency, as is the placing of the advertisement in the chosen publication.

Any personnel consultant you engage would almost certainly also use an advertising agency for this purpose, often marking up the agency's price before passing it on to you.

If you wish to hide the identity of your organisation at the advertising stage the advertising agency will gladly incorporate their own address into the text, and will forward replies to you unopened. This is all part of a service, which incidentally should not cost any more than the direct cost of the advertisement would be if you dealt directly with a newspaper or magazine.

Advertising agencies receive commission from the media. That is their main source of income. They may of course charge some extra for the art-work but generally the cost to you will be no more, and maybe even less, than if you dealt directly with the publication.

Key vacancies often attract literally hundreds of replies. Do not delegate the vetting of these to anyone. Instead allow yourself a time limit in which to be impressed enough by a reply to read that CV in full. Experienced candidates keep CVs very brief, knowing that the attention span of the typical reader becomes very limited when faced with two or three hundred applications.

In any case with your experience you should be able to assess after a very short length of time whether it is worth continuing to read. Competition for a key position is very intense if the job is worth having, and the best candidates should be able to gain your interest within a maximum of two or three paragraphs.

Reading them yourself rather than delegating the task, often broadens your own perspective about the job and its possibilities. Often the approach the candidates' express will give you some new ideas that you can incorporate into the job specification, and will always clarify the things you expect in your ideal applicants…

… nothing is static - we learn all the time…

You might of course involve some of your colleagues in the CV vetting process, getting their opinions and observations on the candidates. You will probably want to utilise at least one of them in the interviewing procedure, particularly when they will ultimately be working closely with the successful applicant. There should always be consultation and perhaps collaboration, but not delegation.

SELECTION INTERVIEWING

Interviewing candidates for a job is a very imprecise science. That is why so many apparently self-confident people delegate it, or at least try to involve as many others as possible in the process, thus 'sharing the risk' or spreading the responsibility.

It is often claimed that an interview is an absurd way of undertaking the vital task of recruiting. Such arguments are used all the time to justify the involvement of both the psychometric and other 'scientific' tests lobby and the 'pure' headhunting school of thought. In the latter method of course the job is not advertised, but 'suitable' candidates sought out through a network of industry contacts.

Whatever the arguments for and against, all methods include extensive interviewing as well as the more specialised techniques. No other method has been proven to be more successful than just interviewing.

It must be stated that all recruiting particularly at senior level, has factually a relatively high failure rate, however 'scientific' the techniques involved.

Do not be discouraged by adverse comments about 'intuitive selection'. As a leader you should have well developed intuitive skills as well as analytical and reflective judgement. Those who continually discredit intuition are those who do not possess it to any degree and who do not understand it.

After many years of very intense personal participation in recruiting I firmly believe that the experienced leader, using well-honed instincts and perception, when interviewing with energy and interest, will always produce the better results. No selection method is perfect. The interview is however yet to be superseded, cannot be eliminated, and correctly used is as effective as any combination of other techniques.

By retaining most of the recruitment process the boss will develop an ongoing awareness and a sharpening of the senses that enhance the accuracy of the process. In addition the saving in both consultants fees and the hidden cost of an extended recruitment timescale, will be significant.

Perhaps an even more important benefit results from the early start of the bonding process between the boss and the new team member.

The more contact resulting from the top man's personal control of and involvement in the recruiting process, improves the chance of a successful outcome.

From that correct choice, evolves a 'head start' in working together that starts with the more intensive pre-employment contact.

INTERVIEW OBJECTIVES

The primary objective is obviously to obtain information from the candidate. If this were the only reason then of course the information could have been available from a CV or from an application form.

We must therefore be seeking facts and opinions that are not likely to have been committed to paper by the applicant, or looking for more elaborate explanations provoked by what he or she has written.

It should also be obvious that applicants write down primarily what they want you to know, things likely to put them in a good light. An objective of the interview is to get at the total picture, one that will seldom sustain a one hundred percent flattering image of the candidate.

It is an ongoing cause of concern to me, that this simple fact seems to be lost on very many people who consider themselves good interviewers, and in terms of volume undertaken, are certainly experienced ones.

Such interviewers merely elicit again the information they already have been given on paper. Although the physical presence of the candidate provides a chance to measure such other things as verbal presentation skills, self-confidence, and personal presentation, it seems to me wasting much of the opportunity offered.

Bad interviewers often spend most of the interview simply asking the candidate for information already in their CV. Surprisingly many personnel consultants, often those dealing with very senior positions, fall into this category. What a squandering of time, opportunity, and a great deal of the client's money. Interviews exist to discover the information not provided by the CV.

The main information-gathering objective should be to extract details that the applicant has not already volunteered. Time spent simply going over what is on a CV or application form is time and energy wasted and amongst other things will make the interviewer look silly.

An interview, correctly conducted is an exploration exercise, designed to give you a deep insight into another person's character. What motivates him or her, excites or depresses them, their attitudes to many topics that you find relevant to the position applied for, and observation of how someone conducts himself or herself when faced with a competitive endeavour, which they (hopefully) want to win.
If you do not agree, then I suspect you do not want to lead the sort of team I am used to leading.

Another interview objective is the selling of your organisation to the candidate. You should assume that the very best applicants would be in great demand for their services.

If they are interested enough in joining you to give time and effort to their application, then you must give equivalent effort to promoting yourself and your team in an interesting and attractive light. There is no point in projecting yourself as such an autocratic and arrogant pig that no one with any self-respect will want to work for you.

Additionally a mutual rapport can be established during a successful interview that will initiate the bonding process so essential to good team performance, way ahead of the candidate joining. In effect you are already working together during the interview. Such a synergistic relationship often emerges at the first meeting between strong and able individuals...

... a form of rapport...

PREPARATION

I am continually amazed by the lack of preparation that so often precedes a series of selection interviews. Sometimes such meetings are given no prior thought at all, relegated to almost the same level as fulfilling an appointment grudgingly given to a reluctant salesman in a kind moment, and then resented when the appointed time arrives, with an urge to get it over as soon as possible.

Recruiting staff should always be approached with a seriousness that befits one of the most important functions of any one in a leadership position. You need the best staff. The applicant has gone to much trouble to get to the interview stage and is giving up time to see you. It is a formal and serious situation. In the same way that the candidate should be punctual and courteous in dealing with you, in turn you should behave similarly.

Thought must be put into what you intend to achieve from each interview. Prior to the meeting you should have thoroughly re-read the applicant's CV, noting items that are unclear, and formulating a list of questions arising from the information it contains.

All CVs are more interesting in what they do not say than for what they have written in them. Remember they are the applicant's sales pitch to get to the interview stage - to get to meet you. A CV is the advertising, not the product. You are about to test, to examine the product itself.

As we will discuss shortly, there is more to asking questions than just asking questions! If you are inviting one or more of your colleagues to join you in the interview, as distinct from conducting a separate interview themselves, then you need to establish a degree of discipline amongst yourselves in order not to interrupt or side-track a particular build-up of questions aimed at excavating a specific subject.

COMBINATION QUESTIONING

The most enlightening information is usually arrived at through a thoughtfully constructed combination of questions rather than one or two specific ones. Sometimes you may choose to be a little circumspect in your approach to an important detail, and you do not want your build up ruined by an injudicious comment or enquiry from a colleague.

Predicting this possibility you need to allocate 'areas of responsibility' for the interview with your colleagues.   By all means   share   the   workload, it provides neat little gaps giving time to analyse what you are hearing and to collect your thoughts prior to investigating another point. However you should plan to remain firmly 'in the chair'.

A good team of two or three interviewers used to working together can be extremely effective. However they must truly work together and not each conduct some sort of separate interview. I have no particular preference whether I conduct an interview in the company of colleagues or solo. However where it is desirable to involve colleagues then I feel strongly that it is best done together in one interview rather than as a series of separate ones.

Two or more separate interviews tend merely to be repetitious, collecting duplicate information rather than investigating to a greater depth. A meeting to compare opinions is then required, adding an unnecessary extra level of communication inviting distortion of information slowing the whole process.

They are wasteful of your team's time and also that of the applicant, who may therefore form a negative opinion of your efficiency. Providing you and your colleagues can interview as a team, the single interview pays off significantly in terms of efficiency, the 'selling' of the team to the applicant and the depth of perception that you as a team can establish.

CONDUCTING THE INTERVIEW

Always conduct the interview in pleasant surroundings. Remember the candidate is going to some trouble to meet you and should be accorded the civility and hospitality you would normally extend to a visitor, a guest to your offices. The offer of tea or coffee is always welcome, especially if they have travelled far.

There is a strong opinion that interviews should be conducted on more 'neutral territory' such as a conference room. I do not agree with this, it should be your own office if space and appearance permit. Your office I hope reflects your character and personality in many ways, so why should it not play a part in the interview process?

I once had a very protracted argument with a management psychologist on this subject, and I remain firmly convinced that he was wrong. The argument against using my own office was that it gave the applicant clues about me, that he or she could use in the interview, saying things calculated to please and impress me.

As I regard such observation and behaviour as a necessary part of the armoury of those of us who work in customer oriented businesses, I am encouraged when I see such a tactic used on me during an interview. I use it as part of my assessment of the candidate. But then I am a businessman, not a management psychologist.

Whatever location you use for the interview, make sure your guest is comfortable. Do not be tempted to play any games with the seating arrangements such as positioning yourself with your back against a strong light source, so your face, particularly your eyes, cannot be clearly seen.

I know all the games that can be played. In the old days when smoking inside working premises was permitted - ashtrays were often hidden to see how the candidate coped with the problem of disposing of the ash. Believe me they are not even worth considering. They tell you very little in a business interview.

Go to trouble to make sure your guest is comfortable. Indicate where they should sit - offer tea or coffee. Always ask a few trivial questions about their journey, the weather, or some topical subject to break the ice.

QUESTIONING

Apart from the already mentioned mistake of making the interview a spoken reiteration of the CV, many interviewers simply conduct the meeting as a seemingly aimless chat without much apparent point or direction to their questioning. Before meeting the applicant you must have thought through what you are trying to achieve.

Time and time again I have seen interview questions confined to what jobs the applicant has done, at best a mere extension of information already in the hands of the interviewer. It should be more about how the jobs were done, the knowledge, strategies, techniques, and policies used to do the work successfully.

Having previously considered what you are seeking from the candidates, how do you find whether they meet the requirement?

If you ask someone; "Are you a hard worker?" or; "Can you sell £95,000 worth of personal computers each month?"
… the answer is y are likely to be in the affirmative...

Do you really think that means they are being accurate? At an interview they are in 'sales mood'. Their objective is to be offered the job. They might subsequently refuse the offer, particularly if they have been economical with the truth and cannot risk being found to be lacking on the job.

It is unlikely that you will find very much about someone by simple direct questions. Particularly if it is information they do not want you to know. The art of the good interviewer is in the supplementary question.

SUPPLEMENTARY QUESTIONS

For every question you ask you must be prepared to follow it up with a supplementary one. Although you may start off with a good idea of what your opening questions are likely to be, you can be completely open-minded about the supplementary ones.

These follow-up questions should be triggered by the answer to the preceding one. That is how you find things out in everyday life, but it is surprising how some bad or perhaps nervous interviewers forget to use the technique, and stick to a simple premeditated questionnaire method.

The 'problem' with the supplementary questions is that in order to keep firing them in, you have to 'think on your feet'. When engaged in normal social conversation it is very easy to delve into what your companion is talking about, following each reply with yet another question.

However whilst enquiring into how a stranger undertakes in detail a project, or task that you might not have any knowledge about, the ability to come up, again and again, with meaningful and intelligent supplementary questions, is not quite so easy. It is however vitally necessary if you are to measure whether the applicant knows what is being claimed.

In our jargon-crazy age it is very simple for someone to acquire the 'buzz-words' so embraced by most professions. It is equally simple by insisting on an explanation of what is really meant, to gauge the accuracy of their knowledge. It is the fourth or fifth level of supplementary questions to each primary question that will elicit the most interesting and informative answers.

Like every other worthwhile endeavour, the skilled deployment of probing supplementary questions, particularly in subject areas where you are unskilled, will need thought and practice.

If you persevere the talent will come sooner than you might expect. Most of it is only common sense anyway but, as in so many areas, the so-called experts have woven a shroud of mystique and alleged know-how in order to optimise their own financial opportunities.

Whilst interviewing you will of course be noting how the candidate answers the questions and not just what the answers are. Self-confidence and communication ability show up here. Do not fall into the trap of popular myths concerning appearance and mannerisms.

Often they belong to the 'body-language is everything' school of thought, and there a little knowledge can very much mislead you. Take for example the case of an applicant who retains spectacles on a lanyard around the neck when not actually wearing them. 'Professional' interviewing wisdom maintains this to be an indication of absent-mindedness...
... is this really necessarily so?

It could mean that the person is so organised and efficient that wearing the glasses around the neck provides the quickest and most convenient way of locating them when required for reading. I know several people who use them for this, and not one of them is in the least absent-minded. It might say something about their dress sense or their style, but these are other issues.

HOW - NOT WHAT

Always ask how your candidate did or does things, as distinct from what he or she does. This may seem obvious but it is frequently omitted. It is the only way you will get at whether they know what they are talking about. I could easily say that I am a ships captain, but might not know anything about the job.

Only by being asked for example, how I navigate the vessel, how I calculate its load carrying capacity for differing saline densities in various oceans, or what are the overtaking rules in the English Channel, would any overstatement on my part be detected. It would not matter whether my inquisitor knew the answers, the manner of my replies would almost certainly betray me.

It amazes me how many interviewers, even self-styled 'top' head-hunters, do not ask candidates how they do things, as distinct from what they do. In my dealings with such people I have only once been asked such questions as how I would solve a typical business problem, although I have been bursting to put such knowledge over to them. All the rest disappointingly, only asked for information already on the CV in front of them...
... not very impressive...

Sometimes even when it is obvious that the applicant knows how to do something well, it is worth asking the questions for the opportunities they then give you for asking probing, supplementary ones.

Getting someone to talk in depth about a subject can also give you a little breathing space from your relentless composition of supplementary questions in order to evaluate details of the candidate's normal communication style, as well as his or her ability to generate enthusiasm and interest.

Always make sure you stay firmly in charge of the interview. A strong candidate and a weak interviewer can result in the candidate 'setting the agenda' and running the interview. When this happens the applicant generally puts across only what he or she wants the other person to hear, at best an extension of the CV but more probably a cynical manipulation of the interviewer, telling him what the candidate thinks will impress most.

If you cannot stay in charge of the interview then you probably should not be conducting it, but then you probably should not be the boss either.

By all means test the candidate for assertiveness and even aggression, if they are relevant to what you are seeking. It is easy to do this with a degree of provocation, mild at first, but increasing until you form your opinion.

Never however be rude, the applicant remains your guest for the duration of the meeting, and in any case you are selling an impression of yourself and your organisation. Even if you do not hire the candidate, he or she might one day emerge as a client or customer.

Some minor considerations are avoiding questions that can be answered 'yes' or 'no'. Aim at getting the candidates to express themselves more 'openly'. Do not indulge your ego by talking about yourself.

If the candidate wants to interview you the opportunity will arise in so much as you wish to permit it, when you invite questions probably prior to summarising and winding up the meeting. Remember you are in the chair.

Be very honest about the job on offer. There is always a tendency to oversell jobs particularly to the best applicants. This is a serious flaw and one likely to have very undesirable repercussions when the candidate joins and discovers the truth. Never oversell the job.

Do not however, forget to 'sell' the good points about the job and your team. Even if a good candidate does not accept the job you offer, there may be a next time. In any case people talk and you want the words spread to be as favourable as possible. Always tell the truth about company and job.

Make sure the candidate will depart the interview knowing what has been achieved and where his or her application stands. If you have decided to offer the applicant the job, then say so at the time. You can work out the details later. Give a date when a written offer and details will follow, or fix a date for a meeting if one is needed to finalise things.

If you have decided to make the offer subject to references or other qualification, then say so. If you are not in a position to make a decision having seen others, then say so but give a definite date as to when a decision will be made...
... specify when you will be in touch...

However if you have decided against making an offer, then say so on the spot, do not let someone depart in a state of false hope. If you cannot decide then again be honest about it, giving your reasons.

As previously stated the bonding process of a new team member often quite rightly starts at the interview. Remember the person in front of you could become an important member of your team.

Send them away pleased with themselves, in a positive and enthusiastic frame of mind and believing in themselves.

KEY POINTS

* Recruiting - a most essential task - you are only as good as your team
* Lazy leaders make lousy recruiters - it's too important to delegate
* Delegation to recruitment consultants, usually an abdication of responsibility
* Not taking responsibility for your recruiting is cowardice
* The right recruit could change your life
* Read all the CVs - you will learn something
* Psychometric and all the other aids - still nothing to beat the best interviewers
* Seeing through the CV
* Make sure you 'sell' your organisation
* Learn to enjoy recruiting
* Do not show off at interviews - you're there to learn from the candidate
* Perfect your interview techniques
* Clever questions delve deep - yes/no answers reveal little
* Understand the power of the supplementary question
* Remember your new colleague's contribution starts at the interview - and so does your leadership of them

NINE
Tools Of The Trade

Continuing from the previous chapter we look at areas where the team leader will be frequently involved. As in all aspects of business life there remains scope for individuality in all these areas, and therefore are no hard and fast rules. However there also remains much opportunity for time-wasting, muddle and general inefficiency.

As the person in charge you should provide a lead and an example in undertaking these functions efficiently, and by doing so pass on some of your skills knowledge and ideas, to your team.

MEETINGS

Most organisations have far too many internal meetings. The typical meeting lasts much too long, and usually involves many more people than necessary for the issues being considered.

Whenever I personally undertake a 'troubleshooting' assignment, one of the indicators I can interpret most easily, is what I refer to as the 'meetings factor'. If I find many meetings with a high proportion of the 'management team', involved in them, then I know immediately that I am in the presence of weak leadership.

If many of the meeting are regular ones, 'scheduled' at the same time every week, then I begin to wonder if the company is actually in the business of holding meetings, as distinct from selling computer software or whatever sector they claim to be in.

Most meetings are not necessary. The ones that are essential seldom need all those in attendance. Almost all meetings last too long. Normally people like to attend meetings. It makes them feel important. That is not a good reason for having a meeting. Many bosses include staff in meetings whose presence are not strictly necessary, fearing that to leave them out might upset them in some way. That is not a good reason for having them present. It is also weak leadership.

MEETINGS AS A COMMUNICATIONS FAILURE

The more people attending a meeting the longer it tends to last, irrespective of what is achieved. Often the length of a meeting tends to be directly proportional to the numbers attending. Why should arithmetic come into it?

Meetings also last far too long when they are poorly chaired. When I go into a company and see that they have, for example a regular 'two hour sales team meeting' scheduled for 9.30AM on Monday mornings, I cringe.

Invariably the meeting does not get going until 10.00 o'clock wasting the entire team's time up until then. It is usually a ritual of routine reports trotted out in turn by each person attending, followed up by some feeble attempt to elicit individual commitments for the forthcoming week.

Whilst each participant recites their account of the previous week, everyone else with the exception of the chairman, fidgets, looks bored and is usually totally disinterested.

205

Dissident participants often sidetrack such meetings onto topics that have no place on the agenda. The inability of an ineffective chairman to deal with these, results in further and totally irrelevant time wasting, often degenerating into a cabaret for the entertainment of those not directly involved...

... what an incredible waste of valuable time...

It is a ritual wasting a complete morning, more if travel is involved, for the entire sales team. Try calculating the cost, not just the direct cost, but also the loss of potential business to the company and the loss of time of those outside the meeting who need to, but obviously cannot, communicate with someone inside. Yet it recurs over and over again not just in sales, but in most other divisions too.

Such information reporting can always be done on a one to one basis, not necessarily even face to face. Claimed virtues of engendering team spirit and competitiveness arising from such regular meetings are largely spurious.

Regular scheduled meetings are best avoided. Where meetings are necessary they should be convened on an 'as needed' basis, limited to the minimum essential participants and kept as short as possible.

A 'culture' of avoiding large, long, traditional meetings, should be evolved, so that the necessity for an internal meeting is in general considered as something of a communication failure; and a diversion of time that could have been put to more productive use.

CHAIRING THE MEETING

Before even deciding whether to hold a meeting, consider the following. What is the purpose of the meeting? What is the objective? Is it to exchange information or is it to address some specific problem and make a decision?

If information exchange is the objective then could it not be done in a more cost effective way? Who is really vital to the meeting? Particularly where information interchange is the objective, meetings are flooded with participants that truly do not need to be there.

Often the person - you... convening the gathering is on an ego trip and feels important by being empowered to call such a meeting...
... not a good reason for having it...

So having finally judged a meeting to be the best solution, how do you go about making it effective?

Restrict the numbers to just those expected to make a worthwhile contribution. Anything more than five or six requires serious thinking about. Others you perhaps consider including in case they have information that might possibly be needed, should not be invited.

Think of obtaining the information required in other ways. There always are some. Also exclude those who will merely be affected by the outcome of the meeting. That is not a good reason for having them present.

The outcome can be communicated to them afterwards. Be ruthless in restricting attendance. Do not be tempted to invite people for some alleged 'democratic' reason. Meetings are neither exercise in democracy nor are they intended to be mass entertainment.

Put a time limit on the duration of the meeting. I am amazed how long I hear some go on for. Even an entire day is not unusual. I personally believe no meeting should last more than one hour. I usually try to limit mine to half that time.

The human attention span is notoriously short. Especially mine! I have attended meetings that go on and on, droning monotonously hour after hour. I have walked out of a good many after telling the chairman how he or she was wasting everyone's time.

Most issues can be decided in quite a short time. If a massive fact gathering exercise is necessary it should be conducted prior to the meeting, summarised and the relevant facts concisely presented.

The chairman should organise this prior to the meeting. If this 'cannot be done' because of the urgency of the situation, the meeting should be put back to allow facts to be collected from the relevant individuals. This enables a certain cooling of the drama usually associated with such 'emergencies'. When the facts are then deliberately gathered in this way, a more considered solution is likely to be arrived at during the subsequent meeting. It takes no longer...
... it is however more effective...

Having a set duration of a half to one hour for your meeting, prepare an agenda. If time allows, circulate it to those attending. If not incorporate it into your opening statement. Start by outlining the objective of the meeting and the time allocated to each item. State the purpose very simply and very clearly for your own benefit as well as for the others in attendance.

You will of course have made sure there will be no interruptions to you or anyone else, whilst you are all together. There is nothing more distracting or farcical than taking calls or attending to messages during a meeting. Yet I know some directors who positively encourage their secretaries to interrupt. They think it impresses the others...
... what prats...

KEEP IT STRONG - KEEP IT SIMPLE

Proceed rapidly into the business to be discussed. Involve everyone, insist on hearing from each of them - stress each individual's importance and the value you attach to his or her contribution. If they appear reticent, if they genuinely have no opinion to offer, then what are they doing there in the first place? Do not allow anyone to ramble or wander off the point. Furthermore do not permit anyone to go into irrelevant levels of detail - in the end it will help them...
... apply the same rules to yourself...

Ruthlessly test levels of understanding at frequent intervals so that everyone is clear as to what is being said and what is being agreed. Deal with any disagreement by insisting the dissenter proposes an alternative and is not just objecting without any clear reason.

All the time keep everyone to the point of what is on the agenda. Keep to the objectives. Continually mentally review the importance, the significance of the discussion. If at any stage it descends to the mundane or the trivial then either the meeting is going on too long and is losing its purpose, or you are chairing it badly.

If the agenda proves too large for the time available, reschedule another meeting if any remaining points are important enough to warrant it. The sequence of your agenda should of course have considered the most important issues first when the attention span of those present is likely to be at its height.

Make sure you do not allow anyone else to 'hi-jack' your meeting. If they are able to do that it should call into doubt your qualification to chair it in the first place.

In winding up, summarise briefly but strongly what has been achieved and what has been agreed.

Again ruthlessly test everyone's understanding. Most important, send everyone away feeling they have contributed to or benefited from the meeting. Test that this is so. If they have not contributed or benefited, then again, what were they doing there? Keep it all simple, strong, concise and objective.

DEALING WITH THE CAREERS OF OTHERS

One of the great responsibilities involved in leading an organisation or a large team is the effect you can have on the careers of those reporting to you. With their career forming such a pivotal role in most people's lives, you are at a minimum able to affect their short-term standard of living, and in some cases in a position of influence that can have a lasting and overwhelming effect on someone's life. It is a responsibility not to be taken lightly.

We all pay lip service to the career development of those we are in charge of. But what does it really mean? Are we really that worried about what our colleagues will be doing in twenty years time, or are we just conducting a public relations exercise aimed at short-term exploitation. As in so many business situations the words can be very different from the truth.

There are many bosses who cynically promise the earth, but sufficiently far off in the future, in exchange for working your fingers to the bone and your immediate undying loyalty. It is expedient, and no doubt justified in the boss's mind at the time. We have probably all done this at some stage, but is it moral? Is it right to play upon the ambitions and loyalties of someone who probably looks up to you, is less experienced, almost certainly far less cynical, and far more trusting?

I am not the one to pass judgement on this issue. It is for each individual to decide for himself or herself. I will only comment that it is all too easy for those of us in a position of power over those we lead, to exploit their hopes, needs and dreams, not least their ambitions. I know where I draw the line. You must think carefully and decide how far you are prepared to go.

Work is a transaction. We exchange our effort and skills for the means of surviving. Some jobs obviously provide a better level of 'survival' than others. Ambitious people are driven by reasons of financial 'need', or reasons of character or personality, to continually seek more power and or more money.

For many money and power are to a large extent interchangeable. If you have power, you can use it to obtain financial gain. If you have money you can use it to buy influence, in short, power.

It is perfectly right for the leader of the organisation to utilise the ambitions of those led - in exchange for greater efforts. Work as we have already discussed is merely a transaction - and people come away from deals more satisfied if thy feel they have benefited from the outcome. There is little distinction between effort and commitment...

... the two are closely related...

I do however believe that unrealistic ambitions should not be encouraged. Apart from the morality involved, it is just not good sense or good leadership, to promise or encourage something that cannot be delivered or is unlikely to materialise.

I am a however a great believer in being scrupulously honest in what I promise my team. It might cause much short term disappointment and has led to the loss of some good people when they disagreed with my assessment of their abilities - or were frustrated by my inability to provide the opportunities they deserved.

In the long term I believe this policy has gained more than it has lost. Even if the individual in question is deceived by a promise you are unlikely to fulfil, there are inevitably others observing from the sidelines, who see cynical manipulation for what it is and will cease to trust you.

A reputation for straight dealing in these matters has an incalculable worth.

FREQUENT APPRAISALS

Most people like to know how they are getting on in any endeavour in which they are involved and which is important or interesting to them. This need is as equally valid when applied to a game such as golf as it is to work. We are competitive animals.

Often I find an attitude exists, along the lines that if nobody is complaining, then things must be going reasonably well. Subsequently when someone's work deteriorates or they resign, it is taken as a signal that maybe things are not so good after all and 'something has to be done'. This usually results in a round of panic reviews followed by expedient salary increases. Of course by then others will have been casting glances at the job adverts and there will probably be other resignations in the pipeline.

Everyone's performance must be reviewed at intervals no greater that every six months. In general I prefer a gap of only three or four months - although it might not be practical to review pay with such frequent appraisals. However we are talking about a review of performance not necessarily a person's pay. Individuals need to know how their efforts are being viewed. If they are doing well they will realise the six monthly or yearly pay review is likely to be favourable.

Sometimes where a category of specialist staff is highly sought after and demand exceeds supply, it is necessary to formally review salaries at an unusually frequent level. In the early 1970's there was a tremendous shortage of computer programmers and their pay levels were escalating almost monthly. By initiating a policy of reviews every four months, I was able to limit the attrition rate amongst my staff.

It did not actually cost any more. On an annual basis it worked out the same. Not surprisingly the possibility of three, albeit smaller increases instead of just one annual one worked wonders. Just as soon as a programmer had got used to one increase, he or she was face to face with the possibility of another.

It was hardly worth them 'playing' the job market, as the chances were by the time they started at a new company, their salary with us would have risen to a level comparable with any new one. And four months later they could get more again. It obviously did not stop genuine 'career' moves, but it prevented much job-hopping just for a few pounds extra.

The fact remains that very frequent performance reviews are essential if you wish to develop an individual's full potential. To do them you must of course, have in place some form of performance monitoring. This will vary from job to job and is well outside the scope of this book. How you conduct the appraisals is very relevant and will form a fundamental part of helping people believe in themselves.

SERIOUSNESS

Conducting an appraisal should be approached with a high degree of planning and thought. It should never be trivialised or relegated to a low priority. You might think more important events have materialised to justify rescheduling such a meeting, but such an attitude is unlikely to be appreciated by the person you are appraising.

There are many and varied techniques of recording performance. Many jobs such as selling have the benefit of a direct measurement of performance achieved from the sales figures. A credit controller might be judged by the cash collected, a bricklayer by the number of bricks laid, as well as the aspects of their work that are maybe more obscure. I have always believed in evaluating these important factors that have no direct quantative input, with a comparatively short list of headings relevant to the individual's work.

This list is first divided into two, the first half reflecting varying personal characteristics that affect performance. Items on this section include communication skills, ability to deal with others, willingness to delegate, amount of initiative demonstrated, and so on. The second half of the list is devoted to the technical aspects of the work and will of course vary enormously from job to job.

The entire list contains no more that about fifteen or sixteen points. Each of these is then or will be graded on a scale from unacceptable, then poor, average, better than average, through to excellent.

Simple, but effective…

Two independent assessments are prepared on each individual being appraised, one by their immediate supervisor and the other by the supervisor's boss. Either or both conduct the face-to-face appraisal with the team member.

The apparent ambiguity here results from the highly geographically dispersed operations that I was involved in, making it often impossible for all three individuals to be together readily in a suitable time frame.

SELF-OPINION

At the appraisal meeting the team member being appraised would be invited to verbally self-appraise using the format of the written appraisal and the comparisons would obviously be discussed. This contrasts with the popular practice of asking for a written self-appraisal. I have found that in practice this creates too much tendency for 'tunnel vision' in the person being reviewed, resulting in much greater resistance to accepting criticism.

After having been subject to previous reviews of this nature a certain amount of mental preparation will inevitably take place destroying much of the accuracy of a spontaneous reaction. Self-assessment is seldom as rigid when expressed verbally as when it has been committed to paper.

I have noted that even quite serious performance shortcomings can be addressed comfortably and without embarrassment when approached in this way. Very few people are unrealistic about their abilities and performance when operating in a close team environment, where the team leader is seen to be closely involved.

It is important to address performance problems openly and discuss them in a non-confrontational way. On too many occasions, performance problems are approached with an expectation that there will be a dispute leading to confrontation, which in turn will become unpleasant and result in a further deterioration.

The common sense approach of providing each individual with a frequent opportunity for comparing their self-assessment with one from their leader on a face-to-face basis is in my experience by far the best way of avoiding situations leading to strongly entrenched differing views. A mutual plan for rectifying the performance problem can then more easily be established.

PERFORMANCE PROBLEMS

Where a serious difference of opinion exists take care not to let it escalate to a position where it becomes almost impossible to rectify. As leader you are responsible for the performance of your team.

If someone is not working to an acceptable standard you must accept some blame. Although you might not have recruited that particular person your role in directing, providing training, and overall quality control, will play a part in any under-performance.

Always set up a constructive dialogue and resist any tendency you may feel to set up a catalogue of the other person's faults. Involve yourself by sharing the blame - it is a tactful strategy and it helps maintain the self-esteem of the person you are dealing with. Together you are not getting it right. Together you will rectify things, and start to put it right.

Nobody wants to appear incompetent, but if treated in an insensitive way or not offered constructive help, they will often retreat into an attitude where they cease to care, and simply muddle along until they find another job or the situation is resolved for them.

If an individual's performance has reached the stage where it is considered irreversible, or some overall objective means that more resources cannot be dedicated to rectifying the situation, then a decisive speedy dismissal is almost always the best solution.

Seldom, when it becomes obvious that someone has to go - is there anything to be recommended for protracting the decision.

It is usually in everyone's interest in concluding it as quickly as possible.

The affect on the rest of the team caused by indecision regarding what has become an obvious requirement for sacking must now take priority.

More indecision is displayed by delaying a dismissal when its need is apparent to almost everyone involved, than from probably any other single leadership matter. Delaying a dismissal when its need has become obvious is a common and serious failure of leadership.

All appraisal meetings should include a discussion on the subject's hopes and ambitions, and how or whether there are promotion prospects in the offing. There is currently a fashion for the boss to ask along the lines of: "Tell me what your ambitions are and I'll help you to achieve them". It sounds good, but in my opinion this is usually just so much 'bullshit'.

Companies and bosses do not exist primarily to enable every member of the staff to become managing director; they are there to give shareholders a return on their investments. Most people express fine ambitions and should not be encouraged to understate them.

The reality is that most will fall far short of their stated ambitions. You do them no favours by leading them on when it is unlikely they will be able to achieve them. By encouraging false hopes. Hence my scepticism about the approach quoted above.

It is far more useful to mutually explore your team member's realistic career steps for the foreseeable future. This is where your help and guidance are of importance. Spelling out what is possible and what they have to achieve so as to get there. Keeping it to realistic targets, and suggesting skill development that you both believe can be achieved.

In any case business changes so fast (or should), so that those ambitions that are too focused tend to become obsolete after a year or so. What should be encouraged is a general vision of the level to which the individual can aspire.

Maintain at the same time a sense of opportunism and the belief that success for the company will bring many opportunities that cannot as yet be identified.

CATERING FOR AMBITION

One of the problems in building up your team of the very best people is accommodating the very real aspirations that they are entitled to hold. It is one of the major leadership problems. In the short term the temptation is to divert the problem with additional financial rewards. This has some obvious problems in the costs of sustaining the policy, but in any case it will not keep the best of your team happy for long.

Good people will inevitably want the responsibility and the power resulting from promotion, and if you cannot provide that, they will seek them elsewhere.

I know many incidents where the strategy is to deliberately recruit less ambitious staff to avoid this situation, an attempt also to reduce the threat to the boss's own position that the best individuals might pose.

I have already made my position clear. I think it is a good thing if the team leader is always conscious of his or her own permanence (or potential lack of it) - due to the availability of strong talent within the team. It keeps the boss performing at peak.

The requirement to satisfy the realistic ambitions of individual team members is more acute. Very few companies are able to expand fast enough to accommodate such ambitions and a certain attrition rate of good people has to be accepted as inevitable.

NO 'YES MEN'

There exists a very real danger when a very strong boss has a weak team. The situation frequently leads to a lack of restraint on the leader's excesses, whether they are in the exercise of power or an unjustified belief in their own infallibility...
... megalomania often grows from this basis...

In many cases the exaggeration and abuse of too much personal power drives most of the remaining able people away from the team, either as a deliberate strategy to reduce rivalry, or they go of their own volition. Either way it leaves an even weaker team, giving the boss yet more freedom for mismanagement.

Inevitably further decay follows. A strong leader must have a strong team. It must contain individuals ready and willing to stand up to the leader on the occasions when he or she are clearly seen to be wrong. When the leader's judgement is faulty there is no place for a 'yes man' in the team.

Strong leaders must have strong and able team members if their own full potential is to be realised, and if they are to avoid a possible situation where inevitable lapses of judgement, are carried forward by the strength of their other personal qualities.

Being a strong believer in the advantages of small units bringing benefits from the sense of identity and team spirit they can engender, I was always very ready to split an operation into autonomous units wherever possible. It helps you. Apart from avoiding the building of large bureaucratic empires, it facilitated the delegation of profit centres, structured as subsidiary companies.

Each subsidiary would provide senior positions giving obvious opportunities for competitive growth in products and services, turnover and profits. Unfortunately this will not fit into everyone's corporate plans. Where it can be accommodated, it is an ideal way of providing opportunities for ambitious and talented individuals.

HARNESSING A COMMON ENEMY

Inevitably there are times in all organisations when the general spirit and morale of a team is lower than ideal and it becomes important to change this. Often it is difficult to identify exactly what is the cause. Usually it will be a combination of many things probably combined with one of those cyclic mood changes that all groups experience from time to time.

Obviously if there are internal measures that can be taken to engineer a major uplift of morale amongst the team, these will be carried out within the parameters of commercial sense. However in general such measures do very little more than tinker with the problem, failing to get to the core of it and providing only a short-term lift.

To tackle any widespread malaise amongst the team it is necessary to focus their attention on an 'external enemy'. There is nothing better than a perceived threat to the common good to bring a group together. Sports coaches have always 'hyped' up their teams using this method, and entire nations are similarly goaded into periods of historic and magnificent endeavour when confronted by warfare with another country.

Politicians are also adept at this strategy, conjuring up various 'bogeymen* associated with the opposition and its policies in order to rally their own supporters.

Despite such widespread employment it remains a useful and important technique.

Commerce of course can often be considered a form of warfare with your organisation fighting for its survival against its competitors. If you have not yet firmly embraced that truth you are unlikely to remain the boss for long. However it is surprising how often this fierce competitive focusing is allowed to slip, as those in leadership positions within an organisation become lazy, careless, complacent, or a combination of all three.

Invariably if there is a lowering of overall morale, it coincides with a period when the company is not concentrating its full corporate firepower on destroying its competition - a time when the morale of its leaders is also depressed. The antidote however must again lie with you. Enthusiasm must be generated and a campaign of excitement, determination, and endeavour promoted.

Spell out the threat posed by the competition and its very real effect on the organisations future health, and consequently the welfare of your team. Many people tend to lose sight of the overall corporate objectives whilst immersed in the day-to-day problems of their jobs.

You must not let them lose sight of what their overall objectives are. It is not easy to effectively focus everyone's mind on the common enemy all at the same moment. It requires much time, effort and skill. There will always be ways of achieving it however, and it will pay dividends in bringing together your team, improving their morale and restoring them as an effective unit. Use the common enemy to rally your 'troops'.

NEGOTIATING

The word 'negotiation' often conjures up the wrong meanings. For too long it has popularly invoked images of confrontation and adversarial conflict. Decades of well-publicised battles between strong trade unions and entrenched employers fuelled a typical image of negotiation, particularly between 'boss' and 'worker', to be inevitably traumatic and mostly concerned with severe differences over pay and working conditions.

This image is totally misleading. We all negotiate at frequent intervals, in reality on a daily basis. Much of our 'negotiation' takes place as a part of normal dialogue and discussion with colleagues, and is considered merely a part of planning, setting targets, agreeing a course of action etc. Although not graced with the title 'negotiation' nevertheless much of which takes place is precisely that.

AN IMPORTANT DIFFERENCE

Because of the popular view that negotiation tends to be an adversarial activity, it is important to remember that negotiations within the team environment are mostly different from those with an external agency such as a client or supplier on one essentially vital point. You are both on the same side.

You are both supposedly aiming at the same objective. You have the same ultimate interests in common. This may be a difficult viewpoint to sustain when locked into a major difference of opinion over for example salary, but it should never be a factor that is forgotten, and is one, which you can return to as a reference point.

Another important aspect to remember is the relative power of the parties involved in the negotiation. When dealing, for example with a client, providing you want to retain their business, their client status gives them many advantages in terms of leverage.

In the final analysis you need their business and are therefore likely to make concessions to keep it. You - when dealing with suppliers of course can use the reverse role. Therefore seldom are negotiations on an 'equal' basis.

When negotiating with your own staff such 'power' advantages are far more complex. On the surface the employer has the power, being able (subject to the complexities of employment legislation), to hire and fire, but most definitely to reward and promote. The employer is also able to 'punish' in many ways, such as withholding promotion or assigning the less attractive tasks.

The realities are of course far more obscure. An easily replaced employee has only a fraction of the bargaining power of a difficult to recruit specialist vital to your most important project, when it comes to pay negotiations. A secretary who has worked with you for fifteen years, knows your moods your style, understands your reactions to most situations, is far more likely to persuade you to re-equip with new desks and re-decorated an office than someone who joined only   a month previously.

Internal negotiations, those with members of the team you lead are likely to be numerous and varied, punctuated often with subtle maybe unvoiced influences, relationships, and 'payments' for deeds past.

Such negotiations invite corporate politics, favouritism, and demonstrations of power.

Many management psychologists treat them on the same level as external negotiations. This is wrong. I regard them as far more complex and subtle than that, being an important and visible part of your leadership skills.

There are many theories, studies and teachings on the subject of negotiation. The very proliferation and variety of these uttering combine to confuse the subject, which however important, is like so many others mainly a matter of common sense and very much a hostage to individual personality and style.

To negotiate is to seek agreement between two parties, commencing from a starting point of differing requirements. I am not advocating a particular theory or method of procedure, but offer a few common sense guidelines around which to build your own personal style.

Negotiation in this context is confined to the leadership role in dealings with other members of your team. In doing so your use of your own status, image and power, will inevitably have a psychological effect on the others...

... you should always be conscious of this and use such power wisely...

The tactics of the bully are unfortunately, sometimes unavoidable but they are never desirable. They do not build teams or command respect. Rule by fear does not create loyalty. In negotiation avoid their use.

IN PROGRESS

Consider a typical situation where one of your team is attempting to influence you in some way that is running contrary to your wishes, such as a major change in working conditions.

Firstly be a good listener. All negotiations have to start with two differing positions. Get the other party to explain their position as comprehensively as they are prepared to do.

If possible let them present their entire proposal before you even begin to state your opinion. Ask questions aimed at getting the other party to expand and expose their position even further. If they are skilled negotiators they will resist this process. Most people like to hold something back, not wanting to use up all their ammunition in the first skirmish.

It is in your interest to know as much of the other's strengths as is possible before you make your views known. Part of your skill will lie in extracting as much of this information at the beginning of the proceedings, whilst resisting your natural urge to put forward your own point of view. It is a sure sign of the inexperienced negotiator - rushing over-eagerly into putting forward his or her own arguments.

When you have extracted as much information as is practicable, summarise it back to the other party, seeking their confirmation that you have understood them fully. As well as its obvious verification role, it gives you time to fully digest the information especially if it contains anything new to you.

Now challenge any inaccuracies in their statement. Do so on a purely factual basis. Do not ridicule or insult in any way. Apart from the offence caused it would merely dilute logical debate by bringing irrelevant skills into play. I am assuming that no company exists out there in the business of ridicule and insult. It is best left to authors.

CLARITY

Test the arguments of the other party to determine which are the points they feel strongest about. If you have not succeeded in getting them to present their case in full by this stage, use your summary to initiate more questions aimed at achieving this. By using your summary to demonstrate your grasp of their case, you are likely to be 'rewarded' by some of your additional questions being answered.

It is a common characteristic in a 'dispute' situation, that if the 'opposing' party seems to be coming around to our way of thinking, even if only by appearing to listen to and understand our reasons, then we encourage them with a 'reward'. Understand and use this to your advantage.

Make sure the central issue is kept firmly in sight. If you are just being used as an audience for a whole bag of unrelated problems, then recognise that you are not in fact in a negotiation but in a conference or a meeting, and instantly redefine it as such, and immediately obtain such recognition from the others.

ANALYSE

Consider the range of points that have been put to you. Try to identify which ones are more important to the other party, mentally separating them from those of lesser importance that have maybe been included to add 'weight' to their case. These could well be 'sacrificed' as a concession to you during the bargaining - a trade-off in exchange for concessions from you. They probably will have been included precisely for that reason.

If you can isolate them you will be better prepared to recognise their true value or lack of it. You will therefore be more likely to save any concessions that you are prepared to make, to exchange for things you value more highly than the deliberately included expendable ones of the other party.

EXPLAIN...

Do not open your presentation by disagreeing with or disputing the other person's proposals. Instead explain the strongest items of your position first. Be open, honest and concise. You are trying to impress them with the strength of your position. Do not fall into the strategy of reserving some of your reasons and points...
... hoping they will prove of value later...

If your case is strong, then show it. Focus the attention of the other party on its strengths, and then lead them into recognising why you find their position one you cannot agree to. Initially attempt to sway them with the quality of your position rather than the weakness of their own. In doing this you offer a more face-saving route towards settlement.

Frequently check that you are being understood and be prepared to regularly repeat and summarise your strongest points. Where inevitably you have to openly disagree, reiterate the common objectives that you both share as members of the same team, and how such team objectives should have the overriding priority. This is unlikely to prove conclusive, especially in areas affecting individuals as personally as their salary, but it will serve to remind all present of the bonds and responsibilities you all share, and help to elevate the discussion away from the personal level.

DISAGREEMENT

When you disagree, gently introduce the other party to it by preparing the way for outright declaration of disagreement with a comprehensive list of the reasons for it, rather a than stark statement that you disagree.

That latter option is bound only to reinforce their resolve. Continue openly exploring and testing the strengths of their arguments. Instead of just rejecting those that you do not agree with, ask for explanations and yet more explanations.

It is amazing how the act of explaining something down to its most detailed level can undermine many positions, showing them to be based on what it is hoped can be achieved rather than what is feasible or logical.

By meeting a proposal with a series of questions, rather than the outright rejection which the other party has probably steeled themselves to receive, often takes the steam out of the more militant reaction they have prepared as a follow up to your anticipated reaction.

Their response is thus unlikely to be well prepared, if prepared at all. You will already have presented yourself as far more reasonable than expected, and will probably be rewarded with possibly immediate concessions to your point of view.

Keep the central issue and the over-riding objectives at the forefront at all times. Do not threaten or promise sanctions if at any stage you begin to lose the argument. The fact that you are the boss will be obvious enough to the others, and in any case you will hopefully still be working together when the issue is resolved.

AGREEMENT

When agreement has been reached efficiently summarise it and make sure it is understood all round. All too often an unsatisfactory negotiation is concluded with all the participants leaving the meeting thinking they know what has been agreed, but in reality all with a different version of the proceedings.

The end result will be a misunderstood situation that cannot hold together, and which will require further negotiation made more difficult by the failure of the earlier round. Obviously the results of negotiations should be documented as an essential test of understanding and a reminder of what has been agreed.

At all times remember you are dealing with your own team - people of vital importance to your own ambitions and success.

If your team members are the right ones for you, then all of their proposals should be treated attentively and with respect. Use any negotiations with them to further reinforce the mutual interest you all share in their success and welfare.

Use the situation, not for the demonstration of your superiority, but to promote their self-belief and sense of contribution. You will be able to turn potential confrontation into yet another opportunity to participate in developing your team into an even more effective unit.

SETTING TARGETS AND OBJECTIVES

Many targets are set out of a need to achieve a certain level of performance. The obvious one concerns the profitability of the company, or if for example a government department or suchlike, some meaningful level of performance. When a company is already profitable such a target can be readily expressed as a growth factor. If the company is losing money it might simply be the performance required to guarantee survival, and as such could be completely unrealistic but created out of desperation.

If the people who have been set the target or objective do not think it can be achieved it becomes meaningless, an object of ridicule and derision, totally counterproductive. Unfortunately many of these targets exist, usually set by accountants or strategic planners, and based on some externally driven perception rather than mutually accepted and agreed as part of a team effort.

This subject follows very naturally on from the last section concerning negotiation. The best targets, the most achievable objectives - are often ones negotiated within the team environment. Consequently they are the ones that everyone believes in and consider reachable.

People are not fools. They rapidly see through unrealistic targets, lose interest in striving towards them, and usually end up putting in a performance inferior to the one that would have been achieved if the goal had not been set in the first place.

Very often it is extremely difficult to identify what is a realistic objective to set. This is particularly true when attempting a project that has not been done before.

When this is the case, attempts must be made to locate data based on activities that most closely correspond to the one being planned. Very little in life is totally unique and interesting parallels usually exist somewhere.

After whatever available information has been considered and added to the equation, some idea of the scale of the task should begin to take shape. Then estimate the most optimistic target that could be achieved. Follow that with an estimate of your most pessimistic projection.

As the reality is likely to be somewhere between the two, a reachable target will now be easier to formulate. If such has been estimated with the involvement and agreement of your team, and it meets all the other criteria such as cost and timescale, then it stands a good chance of being tackled with enthusiasm and subsequently achieved.

All team members working towards a target must obviously be provided with a system of monitoring and feedback. It is no good relying alone on the satisfaction or perhaps financial rewards derived from achieving it. Additionally it is essential to have some stages of satisfaction and reward along the way. We all need frequent encouragement.

REALISTIC AND OBTAINABLE

Targets must be realistic and obtainable. They must be clearly communicated and preferably mutually established. Measurement must be ongoing and subject to rewarding in stages. The more the team become used to working to such disciplines the better they get at it, and the more they want to continue working that way.

As leader you will be using the system to again show the individuals in your team how they can develop and expand their talents, and to contribute ideas and suggestions to the project. The more you intelligently involve as many of the team as possible, treating everyone as a major contributor, the more they will learn to contribute. In the end it becomes an addiction, and everyone benefits.

Even when a target is substantially underachieved, providing it has been correctly led, and all the measurement processes retained, much will be learned at both corporate and individual level. Lessons that should be put to constructive use to benefit future endeavour.

Nothing, not even failure, is wasted if the team is well led and controlled. Every event can be fed back and used to improve future methods and performance.

It is here that your skill and perseverance as a communicator will pay dividends. Many others will be extremely demoralised by apparent failure, even if it is not their fault, but simply the result of an unrealistic target.

Your leadership ability is essential in such a situation to focus their belief into an appreciation of their own contribution. Get them to realise what they have extracted and what they have positively learned from the exercise, and how to convert it into longer-term benefits. Apparent failure can then be turned into individual success, with a subsequent boost to their self-confidence and self-belief.

TRAINING

This is a subject that I find myself viewing with certain ambivalence. Everyone from the great and the good of the political establishment through to the armchair experts who have never even run a whelk stall, clamour with a boring unanimity for more training and yet more training. Thus training is seen to be the answer to all our ills, from the shortage of skills to the inadequacy of management, and our failure to compete successfully in today's world.

This belief that training is the holy grail of achievement is nowhere more plentiful than amongst the aspiring leadership ranks. I cringe when I find, and it is quite a regular occurrence, the entire board of directors of some medium sized company ensconced in some (always) expensive hotel for several days, leaving their teams with a clear view that no one is in charge of the 'shop'.

Maybe their companies are so efficient and problem free that such mass absenteeism by the entire board does no harm, delays no decisions and actually inspires the remainder of the team. If they do in fact run such examples of perfection, a cynic may be forgiven for wondering what they themselves need to attend expensive training courses.

The truth of the matter is that training is a major industry and growing. I am indeed a beneficiary from its momentum through the sales of this book. However it also is subject to the 'invisible suit of clothes' syndrome. Many believe it is right because, as in so many other areas, they are told it is so.

Even when their own intelligence and perception tell them what they are told is not real, they still swim with the tide of opinion rather than risk ridicule by appearing a maverick.

I believe in training but I believe far more deeply in experience. Practical experience will inevitably beat theory, particularly when combined with the self-confidence borne from knowing it will work through having done something similar before.

THE WORDS BUT NOT THE TUNE

The extreme comparison of this takes place in the cockpits of aircraft. When one of the engines is on fire and the navigation aids have failed, and it is flying in the middle of a severe thunderstorm, I would every time prefer to know that the captain is an old-timer who cut his teeth on a Tiger Moth then flew Lancasters over Berlin, than a youngster with a first class honours degree and most of his experience on a computer driven simulator.

I apply the same virtues to running companies - all too often too much faith is vested by the shareholders in someone with an MBA who knows the words but not the tune.

Train by all means, but do it to supplement experience and not as a substitute for it. Do not bend to calls for training from those whose motives may not comply closely to the team's objectives.

Much training is the result of giving in to pressure, rather than carefully considered planned career development. People are often sent on training courses to 'keep them quiet' or as a reward for some achieved target. If this is the case it must be seen as such and not confused with some higher ideal.

Often attendance at trade conferences and exhibitions is in a similar category as unjustified training. Most industry sectors indulge themselves so frequently with their various trade functions that attendance for many becomes a ritual, and not the business necessity usually claimed.

The genuinely productive and busy often shun these functions, having seen them for the time wasting that regular attendance so often is. Again a case must be made for visiting them sparingly. They have become a growth industry in their own right and it is altogether too easy to pretend to justify them on the grounds of 'having to be there'. It is an evil in a similar category to an overdose of meetings.

EXPERIENCE

The more condensed and concentrated the training the less effective it becomes. Learning new skills is not a matter of cramming knowledge into a brain. The most effective ways of training involve careful interleaving of each training module with some practical experience to consolidate it.

Theory and simulation are useful only up to a point. They lack the feel of the real thing and the excitement generated by success or failure in a real life situation.

The majority of training courses are only a part of the process of acquiring new skills. It is essential that they be then implemented with a high degree of determination. Very few courses can guarantee that the knowledge they impart can be put to effective use.

Normally a considerable amount of time and effort, coupled with perhaps some organisation changes have to take place before the effectiveness of the training is realised. Almost always it will take some time before the beneficiary of new knowledge or skill will get 'up to speed' in using it.

CASUALTIES OF THE 'INFORMATION AGE'

New technology, particularly for those not brought up in today's computer culture, provides overwhelming pressure for training. Even this however is often misplaced. There are many still around, hoping their retirement will arrive before they have to come to grips with a computer system.

For them enforced training is not merely a waste of time and money but a sentence of misery and a probable overall reduction of their effectiveness.

The introduction of modern information technology systems is at best requiring major changes in organisational thinking and invariably a lengthy period to acclimatise and consolidate. To force it upon those who are not likely to use it correctly or whose training needs require a completely different more sympathetic approach is to misuse and misunderstand a training requirement.

Consider training needs on a strictly individual basis, conceding it almost grudgingly, treating it as a privilege and not as a right. I realise this is a highly controversial statement, but it is born from frequent observation of the counterproductive results occurring when training is too readily available or provided on an indiscriminate basis.

Make sure you control the training of your team, and that training does not assume a life of its own as it does in so many organisations. Always use it as an aid to contribute to the acquisition of experience…
… in the long run it is the experience that will count most…

KEY POINTS

* Meetings - most are unnecessary - almost all are too long
* An organisation's efficiency is often inversely proportional to the time their staff spends in meetings
* Meetings must be chaired ruthlessly
* Cynical manipulation destroys team trust
* Review performance at least twice per year
* Share the blame for poor performance
* Structure into centres to accommodate ambitions
* Use common enemy to rally your 'troops'
* Negotiation is not confrontation
* Conference, meeting, negotiation - know the difference
* Cut through the fudge - keep the objectives clear
* Resist demonstrating your superiority - always promote team self-belief
* Unrealistic targets are counter-productive
* Very little is original thought - mostly things evolve from historic experience
* Training - no substitute for experience

TEN
Changes

When things appear calm, everything is working well and there are no problems in sight, then is the time to worry. Most of the time when you are in a top job there will be a multitude of things requiring attention, plenty of problems that need to be solved. I firmly believe that a chief executive should not be bogged down by day-to-day activities, but used as a trouble-shooter, a source of inspiration, and a force for change.

Call it a superstition if you like but when everything appears to be going particularly well, I always imagine there is some massive problem about to confront me and which I have not predicted. At least this has the effect of focusing my mind on all the possibilities I can imagine. An exercise in predicting what could happen.

Problems apart, business is or should be, a cauldron of change. When you think you have got it right then is the time to begin formulating your next set of strategies. Far too many companies and indeed whole industries, have reached a position of success and dominance only to fall into a haze of complacency.

While the successful dominant company sits back and enjoys its profits and the adulation of its shareholders, there is always some smaller competitor with less to lose, employing a creative and energetic approach aimed at making greater a penetration into the market.

Recent history of the British manufacturing industry is infested with such failures, whilst that of our far eastern competitors is studded with successful examples of innovative change.

COMPLACENCY KILLS COMPANIES

Most people pay lip service to the need for change but in reality are frightened of it. After thirty years in the computer services industry I have many times witnessed the genuine fear, the real alarm that the introduction of new systems has caused.

Many important potential advances have been suffocated at the proposal stage, not for the many and varied reasons officially given, but due to a deep-rooted lack of understanding of what is involved, and a secret lack of self-confidence by individuals in their ability to survive in what would become a totally different working environment.

Very senior managers have told me that they were dedicated to keeping computers out of their area of responsibility until they had retired. They had no wish to understand the technology. Maybe they privately felt it would be too much for them to understand. Hence they strongly resisted its introduction. We thought dinosaurs were extinct?

With such attitudes it is not surprising that we are rushing headlong towards the status of a 'third world' economy. If anyone thinks the answer lies in training and that I am now offering views at odds with my comments in the previous chapter, then I contend it is education that is required and not training. There exists a massive difference.

It is no good just believing or feeling that the company must develop new products, identify fresh markets and introduce new systems...

... everyone will of course agree...

Many will salute such a philosophy whilst quietly wishing it will go away and not disturb their peaceful routine.

Some of these people will then subvert the processes towards change, several perhaps fearing personal inability to adjust or alternatively worrying in case the balance of power and influence may be altered in some way if change takes place. It is only human nature to want to preserve one's personal interests.

Whatever the reason, if the necessary change does not take place the organisation will suffer. Apart from any direct damage to product ranges, markets and profitability that are likely to occur, there will be a further cost as the more flexible, often brighter members of the team drift away to join more enlightened employers.

Yet you cannot blame those resistant to the proposed changes, unless of course the chief executive is one of them. The momentum that ensures flexibility and change must start from, and be maintained by, the leader of the team.

No one else has the status to guarantee its success. Only good leadership can overcome the inevitable resistance that will be met. That is why it is more a matter of education rather than training.

A PROCESS OF EDUCATION

You cannot train someone who has done a job the same way for thirty years to welcome in a new, alien system, that he or she feels may bring about his or her redundancy. Such acceptance of change can only be engineered by sensitive and skilled leadership, educating the sceptic in how and why the company has to follow that particular path, and what measures will be taken to ensure the minimum casualties.

It has to be done at an individual level and communicated with great understanding, integrity and sensitivity. Any blanket attempt to convey the reasons for the changes is likely to be misinterpreted by those whose jobs, even life-style, appear threatened.

ANOTHER OPPORTUNITY TO LEAD FROM THE FRONT

Overseeing significant change in an organisation is no place for too much delegation. You cannot control such situations by staying in your office and directing others. It is vital you yourself undertake the major communicating of the strategic reasons for the necessary measures.

Only when you have completed that task successfully do you hand over to departmental and subsidiary team heads to supply the more minute details as they affect individuals. Even then you only delegate if the scale or the operation is too great to be handled entirely by you.

Make sure you spell out how you personally will be affected and how you will have to adapt to the changes proposed. Whatever you do, never give the impression that you will be sitting comfortably aloof in your warm snug office whilst everyone else's working lives are in turmoil. Lead from the front...
... from any place else it's not leadership...

MUST BE SEEN TO HAVE A PURPOSE

Beware of change just for the sake of it. Despite the pressures and the necessity for all of today's business to continually overhaul their operations, the proposed changes must be justified by the organisation's overall objectives.

The changes must be 'sold' to the team as a necessary and good thing, even though some members might be 'damaged' in some way by the proposed actions. Obviously there is often a need to introduce incentives in order to help overcome resistance and to lubricate implementation.

Whatever the incentives offered, no significant program of change can possibly be successful if those affected do not truly believe in its benefits claimed. Skilled and open communication is essential to ensure the proposals are seen to be constructive by the majority of the workforce. The effective implementation of change is a test of leadership.

A STATIC BUSINESS IS A DYING BUSINESS

Make sure your views are widely known and that you fully support, endorse, and are in effect the instigator of the changes taking place. A static business is a dying business. Today's world is far too competitive for a business just to remain, as it is - however dominant its existing position appears.

Change often involves initial sacrifice perhaps leading to insecurity and concern. Understanding of such problems must start at the top, as must the clarity and vision that will show any sacrifices to be potentially worthwhile.

CREATIVE THINKING

There is very rarely if ever, such a thing as a truly original thought. Mostly what is claimed as original is in reality an extension of a previous idea, or perhaps the continued evolution, of something already in existence. Try to think of something that is original. I would be very surprised if you produce anything that does not have its inspiration in some existing product or stemming from a past experience.

The virtual impossibility of truly original thought must be understood when considering creative thinking. Far too much despondency is created by frustration caused by inability to produce good ideas.

People generally expect too much of themselves in this area. They often assume that others have a mysterious talent for original thought or at least have complete superiority in the creative thinking department.

Those acclaimed as having such qualities naturally do not deny it. The truth is that most generators of ideas produce them not so much from any god-given creative abilities, but by sheer hard work identifying and enhancing existing methods and techniques.

FAT, DUMB, AND HAPPY

Make a habit of challenging accepted concepts in every field. As a young systems designer, I often asked why something was done in a particular way, I was frequently met with the answer; "It's the way we've always done it".

Many methods had gone unchallenged for decades and no one could give me a convincing reason for their continuance. More frightening still nobody seemed to care, or to be concerned about changing him or her...

... fat, dumb and happy...

I made quite a name for myself as someone full of good ideas that saved money and got things moving faster. Although I did nothing to dispel my growing reputation as an original thinker, what I was doing was not so much producing ideas but merely challenging accepted practice and proposing common sense alternatives.

I was not so much being creative as being thorough. Everything can be improved in some way. Nothing is immune from change. Nothing is irreplaceable. If you lead an efficient and talented team then they will have potential abilities and skills so far not explored. Challenge everything. There are always better ways of doing it.

If you are prepared to put the time and mental energy into continually reviewing all you see around you, and if you have a good grasp of alternative techniques and methods, you will inevitably come up with many good 'ideas' that could benefit your company.

At the same time encourage your team to think the same way. Do not attempt to promote yourself as their monopoly source of ideas. Again you will find yourself having a catalytic effect on others, resulting in the growth of their belief in their own abilities.

CHANGING YOURSELF

We all undergo significant personal development, as we grow older. The challenges and the problems we encounter along the way all play their part in changing our characters, often causing a complete reversal of beliefs we had, or thought we held when we were younger.

In no area is this so apparent than in the leadership of others. Many start their business careers convinced that the answer to everything is to take a democratic vote, go with the majority wish, and all will be well. How quickly we learn that consensus management is the fast track to liquidation as so many of the co-operative experiments of the 1970s proved.

Others believe in the opposite, a completely dictatorial style. However as their careers progress they sooner or later learn that the best, most valuable of their colleagues require handling with more consideration and sensitivity. A process of trial and error, nature's learning process, takes place, and each of us starts to evolve a leadership style we believe is workable for us, utilising our own individual strengths and weaknesses.

If someone claims to have spent a significant time in a leadership role without making some measurable changes in their attitudes and methods, then I treat such boasts with a modicum of suspicion.

Maybe there are those so talented or so lucky, that they can survive a long career in charge of others, without having to adjust their attitudes or change their style, but I doubt it. If such people exist, then I would question whether some introspective reflection leading to a little revision and fine-tuning of their methods, would have made them even more effective…

… we never ever stop learning…

FINE TUNING

As we pursue our leadership ambitions we must at all times be conscious that many of our beliefs, particularly when we are young and relatively inexperienced, are in fact prejudices, myths or misunderstandings.

Take for example the need to dominate. This urge is often very pronounced in younger people thrown early into a leadership role. They see it as an expression of authority necessary to show others who is the boss. It is used to enforce subservience from those in the team. It will cause inevitable conflict with strong team members who, although accepting the command structure might still rebel against the style of leadership being employed.

Consequently, often through expensive trial and error we learn that such expressions of dominance are in reality symptoms of insecurity, a demonstration of inexperience, and a lack of self-confidence.

Leadership can be a very maturing process, and providing you have the humility to always challenge your own style, it is likely only to improve as your self-confidence grows with time.

MENTAL STABILITY

You will have to learn how to handle the pressures of the leadership process. They can be very real indeed, often not helped by colleagues determined to test your toughness and resolve, sometimes prepared to push you to the limits of a nervous breakdown, occasionally over those limits if they feel you cannot cope and that they could offer alternative leadership.

The resilience and comprehension required in this jungle is again something that can be developed over time, providing you know what is happening around you and can condition yourself to handle it.

You must control any sensitivity to personal attack, the deliberate undermining of the team objectives and what you regard as pure trouble making. If you do not occasionally feel some 'pain' then you are probably not giving enough of yourself.

If not naturally ruthless be prepared to develop this quality in order to remove problem people who do not respond to your leadership. We cannot succeed with others all the time and sometimes have to sacrifice someone in the organisation's interest.

Obviously anyone seeking to cause trouble and undermine your position in a way you find difficult to control will have to be removed immediately.

Like a bad apple in a barrel - anything less and you will be thought a weak leader and lose respect from the rest of your team.

LONELY AT THE TOP

When you have become chief executive life can be very lonely indeed. Of course there will always be many willing to keep counsel with you, ready to offer advice. You will realise that everyone has their own motives and reasons, and that ultimately, if you are a good chief executive, you must make your own decisions. It can be a very lonely place. If you have not experienced it you are unlikely to appreciate how lonely.

As long as people work in groups to solve a problem or undertake some endeavour there will be the need for leadership, and there will always be many competing to supply it.

Wanting to run things, wanting power over others, is part of our million-year-old make-up. We cannot deny it and it would be unhealthy to suppress it. Used incorrectly the urge to lead can be divisive and create counter-productive internal competition.

Using one's leadership intelligently can expand the horizons, hopes, ambitions and expectations of those led, by helping them to appreciate and develop their own talents and skills and showing them how to believe more in themselves.

KEY POINTS

*   The time to worry - when all goes well
*   Complacency kills companies
*   Fear of change - lack of self-confidence
* ` Education - not training - the big difference
*   Only the leader can guarantee change
*   No place for delegation
*   Leading from the front more important than ever
*   Change as a test for leadership
*   Fighting Dynamic and Hopeful - or Fat Dumb and Happy?
*   Pain or gain - good leadership will hurt
*   `Chief Executive - the loneliest position
*   `We all need leaders - do you have the guts to be one?

ELEVEN
Eureka moments

From time to time comes a significant event which, when reviewed in the cold light of a future - hopefully more experienced - day, can be seen to have had a profound, perhaps life changing effect on what had followed

I call these Eureka Moments - and one of which still effects me nearly 50 years later is worth recounting here...

A long time ago - as the grey fifties morphed into the bright swinging sixties - when the computer industry was still relatively in its infancy and I worked at programmer the prototype of Europe's first transistorised computer - we often told this joke...
... I recall it as follows:

We have built a super computer. A politician was invited to the opening ceremony. He was given the opportunity to ask it anything he wanted.

The question was: ' Is there a God?'

After much whirling of cog wheels, sparks and a smell of burning - as the machine fused together with others...
... the great answer came back: 'There is now...'

That was more nearly sixty years ago - but now it's becoming all too real - but it will not resemble God...
... a more accurate symbol will be the Devil...

For forty-six years I had forgotten it - the *thing* the idea, algorithm, solution or whatever I chose to call it. Suppressed the thoughts, the very idea itself - the almost science fiction implications of what it would mean to myself, his career and if I were remotely right - perhaps the entire human race.

At that that time in 1965 when, as a young - brilliant almost beyond understanding - computer programmer - caught up in the then vogue for speculating on artificial intelligence, I had spent many a night pondering the concept and the problems involved.

My revelations - the result was the beginnings of a program, a solution so kick-self simple it produced an almost orgasmic surge of excitement in me - combined with acute sleeplessness, a restlessness that I could not control. One that the most arcane and satisfying coding I had ever undertaken could only redeem that...

A few nights work proved the theory. Like in so many seemingly complex - almost impossible problems, the solution in the end was 'why did I not thing of it before'...
... simple almost absurdly so...

A few solitary nights of stolen use on the powerful, for the time, IBM 360, which I had access to, proved the concept and satisfied my immediate desires. But it was the mid sixties and the most powerful machines available only offered a fraction of the power available in the smallest systems we have now.

The logic of the solution was feasible - but the computing power and the human organisation and labour required to serve it and feed it almost endless information was not possible.

253

The solution, coded onto the punched cards of the day was boxed and locked away. Intended to be forgotten but too intellectually and emotionally important to be destroyed - although I was fearful of revealing it to others...

... such was its potential...

Fast forward to now, our time. A recent report claimed a scientist was building the software equivalent of the human brain. It would require the construction of the fastest, most powerful computer ever contemplated or attempted - a frightening prospect in an age when already things had, arguably, gone too far.

My wife argued that like in so much fiction, things could get out of hand, out of control - that the project could mutate into a monster that would have a life of its own - but is it not too late to reverse the exponentially expanding trend - too late to prevent the ultimate slide into a world run by an electronic life form...

... fortunate if humans are retained as pets...

Now, although old - my memories have been awoken - I have contemplated and considered this now that we are in an age when the search for neural systems is re-igniting.

There is a difference and if considered to its logical conclusion it is almost unbelievably sinister. Processing power has grown - is more than exponentially powerful when compared with fifty years ago - when I had stumbled on the problem's solution - but additionally was the ability the machines have to communicate with each other using technology such as the Internet to join together on a worldwide basis...

... the fifty-year-old joke could become reality...

The potential, I realised is infinite - the future, where mankind is superseded by electronic intelligence is tangible. I also believed that an exponentiation in the art of hacking - the breaking into other people's systems by using the same techniques on the hackers but one operated by the electronic viruses would prove formidable.

I found myself constructing a logic where my brainchild would enable electronic communication itself to allow the system to grow and mutate, acquiring the knowledge previously gathered over millions of years of evolution electronically, over a relatively short period of time. A sort of super brain - in control of itself but ultimately far too complex for humans to understand - all powerful. Ultimately it will end the human race - not through war, nuclear weapons or mutations of disease - but through loss of control to the machines.

Consider these analogies:

A electronic whirlpool perhaps - a swirling violence of information sucking in all the data around it - or better still a boundless black hole in space whose insatiable vortex draws in everything around it until it possesses all known matter.

Super Brain will ultimately do all that until human life form becomes its servant, its creature - part of its equipment…
… we will indeed be fortunate if we are still kept as pets…

We do not need the super computer. It is already here - the millions of existing machines with the capacity to communicate with each other - each year vastly increasing in number.

All it needs is the software…
… the solution is simpler than is realised...

Rightly or wrongly - I made a decision to exit the technical side of the computer industry and concentrate on running companies. It was done out of a sense of foreboding and although possibly my decision cost me financially I have not regretted it.

GOING IT ON YOUR OWN

Apart from the obvious requirement of talent, motivation, financial capital, a place in the market - and perhaps a unique selling point - there is an often a forgotten price to be paid in one's personal relation ships - happiness and quality of life. A very high percentage of business start-ups end up with the founder's marriage or private life a major casualty…
… it is a decision not to be taken lightly…

The insidious encroachment of today's employment laws is discouraging many talented people from pursuing their entrepreneurs' bent even to the extent of continuing existing businesses, let alone starting new ones.

Laws, many influenced by Europe's pro socialist tendencies, conspire to deprive firms of productive time through paternal leave, mandatory holiday minima, shorter working hours and many other 'worker's rights'. In addition the compensation culture encourages a plethora of claims, many backed up by the race relations and other discrimination industries.

The paperwork required to remain legal is itself oppressive, detracting from time that could be utilised for more creative activities. Employing other people is now a very unattractive pastime.

Recently there have appeared a plethora of regulations and laws defying common sense and seemingly designed to frustrate the potential entrepreneur. In the main these purport to combat discrimination n the form of sexism, ageism and many other 'isms as well as enforcing undue generosity over things such as sick pay, holiday and maternity leave.

I do not intend to debate these things - I am old fashioned - and there are many ways of avoiding or minimizing the ensuing problems but you do not have to employ anyone to run even a large business. The availability of formidable modern technology plus the coverage of almost any business resource by out-sourcing companies makes it possible for one person to control an empire. The Internet is inspiring a whole generation of startlingly successful new businesses.

Consider also the following: market research, design, manufacturing, distribution, warehousing and order taking, telephone selling, sales by personal representation, administration, accounting and secretarial. All of these activities can be easily sub-contracted or out-sourced, to use modern terminology, leaving the company owner controlling everything from his computer terminal without the risk or worry of employment legislation. Geological proximity is no longer so important - such are the capabilities of current technology. Carefully drafted contracts, themselves written by those traditional out-sourced servants, solicitors, can give more certainty of performance than your own staff.

Forget traditional staff loyalty - instead buy long-term performance by building relationships with customers and your required supplier - remember - you are their customer.

Obviously the magnitude of the regulations affecting the running of particularly people businesses is a massive deterrent. Small businesses seldom can afford the resources in staff needed to keep abreast of all the rules - often suffering from regulations that fall foul of basic common sense.

This deterrent is counter to enterprise - stifling initiative and stilting energy - it does nobody any good - except endless taxpayer parasites that get their pleasure from lording it over us.

Governments have promised to cut bureaucracy and red tape to help stimulate the creation of new particularly small business - following no doubt the many transatlantic examples.

Think about it...
... tomorrow you could be in business...

TURNING POINTS - EVENTS THAT CHANGED MY LIFE

Another of these events, seemingly trivial at the time and perhaps not qualifying as a Eureka Moment, when reviewed much later can be seen as a turning point. Originally minor and perhaps apparently insignificant, in a much wider context, it can be seen to have had an influential and important effect on my later actions.

Recently, while completing my form for the 2011 Census, I recalled this event that happened almost fifty years ago and one that had a important effect on the direction I was later to take.

In retrospect, it was a major turning point.

Sometime in the early sixties, a happy period during which I was performing some very interesting and original programming work until it was abruptly shattered by the failure of the small company who employed me.

I spent a week or two frequenting cinemas and coffee bars - confused and bewildered - my mind racing wildly between practicality and fantasy - thinking intensely about what I really wanted to do and the possibilities open to me.

I had recently met the lady who was to become - and remains - my wife and I felt torn between wanting to impress her, settle down to a 'steady job' - or take a bolder step that might start me on the course to greater prosperity...
... perhaps starting my own small programming business...

I was eager for greater success and financial benefits to buy a home in which to spend the rest of my life with her - a fact which of course was to influence my decision - take a lower risk job with perhaps more financial security or the potentially greater rewards of taking on more unknowns and achieving greater prosperity.

The later step, more money and independence - might well I thought be served by commencing a spell as a free-lance computer programmer - a then very new career being bravely tried by a few 'optimists'. Also, I fantasised about owning what to me would be a special and expensive wristwatch currently being advertised, but well beyond the salary I had been earning.

A small, carefully placed classified advertisement rewarded me with just one reply - from a company processing statistics resulting from the then recent 1961 Census - itself subcontracted from an organisation called The Centre for Urban Studies.

Although it presented me with the potential to earn enough to buy the watch - several small problems presented themselves. I did not consider my O-level mathematics adequate for the statistical calculations required - and I had no experience of using the more advanced model of computer they wanted to use.

But I needed the work and I wanted the money to buy the coveted watch.

With no experience, at the time in quoting contractually - I guessed at a very optimistic one week's work to design, code and test the required program - and I negotiated the price accordingly.

Once the quote had been accepted - I was immediately confronted by two problems. Firstly, never having used magnetic tape storage on an IBM 1401, I faced a choice of wasting time researching the IBM Input Output Control System available - or writing my own machine language version. Lack of time and useful contacts dictated the later course - and that is what I chose to do.

The other - to me more significant problem was the need to code a sub routine to calculate square roots. Of course, IBM had one in its library of macros, but I neither had the time nor the facility to access that.

To me the solution was obvious - write a routine avoiding a mathematical algorithm beyond my O-level maths and instead program a solution using an iterative process of my own design that rapidly converged on the answer.

In the event, this worked beautifully - and I later learned it was superior to the manufacturer's version both in number of instructions used and in its much faster execution time.

It made me feel very proud. At my first attempt, I had out-programmed IBM. It turned out to be the first of many occasions.

The end of my allowed week approached - a judgment day - together with the question of payment. I had quoted as much as I had dared - a lot of money for one week of work. Almost miraculously, the quite complex program worked first time…
… and was put into productive use immediately…

Several, to me, significant things arose from this brief, almost forgotten episode in my youth.

I made a useful amount of money - buying a desired watch that I sill posses and which formed the basis of my prized collection of timepieces.

It gave me the cash I needed, I had beaten, all be it in a very small module of program, the, at the time, biggest computer company in the world, and gained confidence towards my later career starting and running computer service companies. In turn the organisation who had hired me to write the program were so impressed by my doing it in less than one week they offered me a job setting up their embryo IBM programming department.

A fringe benefit was that they so convinced me with their praise for 'my intelligence' that I applied to join MENSA - who measured my IQ at 165 - supporting my view that my lack of formal advanced education was no handicap.

But I took the safe option - the modest security of a regular and fair salary instead of the challenge, perhaps of self-employment and potentially greater riches.

All these things would contribute to enhancing my later life - I still ponder on whether it was the correct decision...
... it had indeed been a turning point...

TWELVE
Conclusions

There has never been a better era in which to develop your leadership potential. Our communication age exposes the limitations of many who run our commerce and society. Every day we are, with a clarity denied us before the multi-channel television age, able to witness the unexceptional who control our lives.

The desire to be led by charismatic, open, inspirational and exciting individuals, in whom we can believe and respect, has seldom been so apparent never so real.

The rarity of those abundantly gifted with natural leadership qualities should provide adequate incentive for the rest of us to work hard on developing the nucleus of qualities that we all possess.

However knowledgeable a person is, sooner or later the best of training and academic qualifications will be found wanting in a real life situation. The realities of winning in face to face negotiation, confrontation and motivation, are miles distant from the theory of the classroom.

In the real world emotions often over-ride intellect - and the more primitive instincts of fear, aggression and survival emerge. The true world, the place of business, politics and public services, is a battleground where specialist knowledge is a common commodity but the ingredients of quality leadership are in short supply…
… opportunities abound…

Most of us start off unaware just how much we can improve our latent leadership talents. Even many of the great leaders of our time did not always set out with their acclaimed charismatic skills in place, having to hone and perfect them over time, despite their self-propagated legends that it was otherwise.

It is stimulating to recognise that many of the qualities we need to lead others such as self-confidence and presence, are assets that grow with age in stark contrast to the physical gifts of appearance and sporting ability.

The best leaders have a complexity of characteristics forming their image and personality. Fortunately most of these can be developed and acquired given the right amount of understanding, hard work, common sense and practice.

Everything from communication ability, self-confidence, through to charisma itself can often be created, and almost always dramatically improved. Nothing will happen overnight but most details will respond to sustained intelligent attention, providing you understand what you are trying to achieve and enough self-motivation.

Most essential is your genuine interest in the needs, life-style, ambitions, and beliefs of those you lead or seek to lead. Mutual loyalty must be one of your paramount objectives, combining it with relentless enthusiasm and hopefully with an injection of excitement, providing the fuel for team endeavour. It soon becomes natural for you to focus the team's communality of purpose and become the one leading them in achieving it.

By creating such an environment you are well on the way to helping others believe in themselves in line with your own growing self-esteem. It becomes a chain-reaction with you and your team stimulating each other in a relentless pursuit of progress and success. As catalyst and initiator of this process your right to leadership becomes irrefutable.

In helping others to believe in themselves not only will you learn about and develop your own latent talents, but also you will naturally become expert at establishing mutual loyalty within your team.

Strengthen this support by fighting for every opportunity to further your mutual interests and being seen to do so. Obviously many associated skills are also needed but they all can be acquired or improved. We all have a nucleus of talents. We all can add value to them with common sense and experience.

Do not persuade yourself or others to make too great a leap in one go. Develop yourself and others in logical realistic stages. It is fine to have ambitions to run the company or indeed the country, but we all need milestones along the way with the next one always within sight, reachable to provide satisfaction and a sense of achievement on which to feed the self-confidence.

Maintain the same philosophy when motivating your team members. It is all too easy to destroy their self-confidence, but building it up and sustaining it needs constant attention and commitment from you. Most of us never reach our full potential because of some lack of self-belief often only felt subconsciously and not admitted. This deficiency is more easily overcome than you think. Work at it and you may be surprised at the results.

In a top job the responsibilities are heavy and the position is usually lonely. The motivation is invariably about power, the key to financial and other rewards.

Not everyone is strong enough and tough enough for the sacrifices, the battles and the stresses involved. Our nature being what it is however, many of us will still strive for the top.

Remember you always need others; you must have a team with you. Show them; help them to believe in themselves, and in doing so they too will taste success. Your own journey to the top will then be smoother and more fulfilling...

Go for it...

End

© Peter Hunter - 2012

By the same author

Fiction

Time Of The Eagle
*

Time Of The Spider
*

The Promise
*

**… too late…
the tallyman…**
*

… death of an Eroticist…

* * *

Articles and stories

both fiction and non-fiction

Wessex Life

*

… cats and other tales…

www.ingramcontent.com/pod-product-compliance
Lightning Source LLC
Chambersburg PA
CBHW060826170526
45158CB00001B/94